Live Long and Die Laughing

MARK LOWRY

W PUBLISHING GROUP™

www.wpublishinggroup.com

A Division of Thomas Nelson, Inc.
www.ThomasNelson.com

LIVE LONG AND DIE LAUGHING

Published by W Publishing Group, a unit of Thomas Nelson, Inc., P. O. Box 141000, Nashville, Tennessee 37214. No portion of this book may be reproduced, stored in a retrieval system, or transmitted in any form or by any means—electronic, mechanical, photocopy, recording, or other—except for brief quotations in printed reviews, without the prior permission of the publisher.

Unless otherwise indicated, Scripture quotations used in this book are from The Holy Bible, New International Version, copyright © 1973, 1978, 1984, International Bible Society. Used by permission of Zondervan Bible Publishers.

Other Scripture references are from the following sources:

The Holy Bible, New Century Version (NCV), copyright © 1987, 1988, 1991 by W Publishing Group, Nashville, Tennessee 37214. Used by permission.

The Message (MSG), copyright © 1993. Used by permission of NavPress Publishing Group.

New American Standard Bible (NASB), copyright © 1960, 1977 by the Lockman Foundation.

Library of Congress Cataloging-in-Publication Data
Lowry, Mark.
  Live long, die laughin' / Mark Lowry.
    p. cm.
  ISBN 0-8499-4204-7 (trade paper)
  1. Christian life—Baptist authors. 2. Lowry, Mark. I. Title.
BV4501.2 .L69 2000
242—dc21

00-047703

Printed in the United States of America

04 05 PHX 10

Contents

Acknowledgments

I HAVE A LOT OF PEOPLE TO THANK, so let me get at it:

I'd like to thank Rick Dinoff for his help in bringing this book to the binders. I couldn't have met the deadline without him. In fact, we didn't meet the deadline. But without Rick it still wouldn't be finished. Thanks, Rick. And I want to thank Ken Abraham, Greg Johnson, and all the folks at Word Publishing for their patience, persistence, and friendship.

I want to thank Scott Davis for having such a wonderful mother (Geneva Davis) who can read fast and who helped me edit this manuscript the night before I had to turn it in.

I promised not only to mention, but to dedicate this book to Martha Bolton. And so I shall. I dedicate this book to Martha Bolton, who is much older than I am.

I want to thank Mom, Dad, Mike, Natashia, Missy, Charlie, all my nieces and nephews (too numerous to mention), friends, Bill Gaither, the Homecoming Family, acquaintances, reMarkables, and relatives close and distant for letting me use you all as fodder for material.

I want to thank you for reading this book. Knowing someone will actually read it makes it worth it.

With a grateful heart, I thank you.

And, most of all, I want to thank God for the precious gift of salvation through Christ. Lord, to experience Your grace makes it worth being born a sinner.

1 Live Long and Die Laughing

I THOUGHT I HAD ATTENTION DEFICIT DISORDER until I met Bill Gaither. He makes me look like I can concentrate. He became the reigning king of ADD, in my eyes, the night we sang at the Grand Ole Opry . . .

It was a Saturday night not too long after David Phelps became our new tenor. When I arrived at the Opry, they ushered me to a dressing room with a star on it. Underneath the star was a sign that read "The Gaither Vocal Band." I walked through the dressing-room door and saw the back of Bill Gaither's head. He was staring at a TV that was sitting on the counter.

I walked over and asked, "How's it going, Bill?"

He grunted.

I continued, "Can you believe we're singing at the Grand Ole Opry—the very stage where Patsy Cline sang 'Crazy' and Hank Williams whined about a cheatin' heart?"

Bill just kept staring at the TV and finally said, "Hey, Mark, don't change this channel. I'm waiting to see a Wal-Mart commercial that's supposed to come on some time tonight."

I said, "'Scuse me? We're singing at the Opry, and all you care about is a Wal-Mart commercial?"

Bill explained that Wal-Mart had just released a commercial featuring Gaither videos. He continued staring at the TV. Just then, Guy Penrod and David Phelps arrived. They immediately asked what was wrong with Bill.

They, too, noticed the back of his head, bald spot glowing, as he stared like a deer in headlights, leaning forward in his chair, slightly drooling . . . all for a Wal-Mart commercial.

A lady told us it was time for our sound check, so Guy grabbed Bill under one arm, I grabbed him under the other, and we led him out the dressing-room door into the hallway that led to the stage. After our sound check, Bill introduced me to Porter Waggoner—a country-music legend and frequent host of the Grand Ole Opry. Bill said, "Porter, this is Mark Lowry. Have you seen our Wal-Mart commercial?" Before Porter or I had a chance to say a word, Bill turned around and walked to the dressing room.

After singing that night, we were all back in the dressing room, shedding our stage outfits and changing into our regular street clothes. I went from the black suit and tie I wore on the show to blue-jean shorts, a shirt, and sneakers. Bill changed from his suit into his vintage khaki shorts (they had holes in 'em) and a shirt he probably bought with his first "He Touched Me" royalty check. David Phelps, who had worn a plastic coat on national television, changed into a nylon number, and Guy Penrod got out of the Civil War rodeo duds he wears on stage and put on a cowboy shirt (one that snaps instead of buttons), complete with ten-gallon hat and a nice, simple pair of chaps, not too obtrusive.

Bill wanted to pray before we left the Opry House. He wanted to thank God for bringing us together and for giving us this opportunity. We got in a holy huddle, put our arms around each others' shoulders, and Bill began to pray. He thanked God for the group. He thanked God for David. He thanked God for Guy. He thanked God for me. (We're supposed to praise Him for our trials, right?)

Bill was really getting into his prayer. I was into it, too. You could feel the camaraderie and support. I had my left arm over Bill's shoulder and my right arm over David's. Guy was on the opposite side of me. About halfway through the prayer, Bill started crying. That in itself is not unusual. Bill cries a lot. Sometimes he'll be quoting lyrics on the bus, and he'll start crying. One time, he was telling me about a song his mother used to sing to him when he was a boy. It was about a dog named Shep, who died. Bill cried when he told me about it. Bill quoted:

Old Shep

When I was a lad
And old Shep was a pup
Over hills and meadows we'd stray
Just a boy and his dog
We were both full of fun
We grew up together that way

I remember the time at the old swimmin' hole
When I would have drowned beyond doubt
Shep was right there
To the rescue he came
He jumped in and then pulled me out

As the years fast did roll
Old Shep he grew old
His eyes were fast growing dim
And one day the doctor looked at me and said
I can do no more for him, Jim

With hands that were trembling
I picked up my gun
And aimed it at Shep's faithful head
I just couldn't do it
I wanted to run
I wish they would shoot me instead

He came to my side
And looked up at me
And laid his old head on my knee
I stroked the best friend
that a man ever had
I cried so I scarcely could see

Old Sheppie he knew he was going to go
For he reached out and licked at my hand
He looked up at me just as much as to say
We're parting, but you understand

Old Shep he has gone
Where the good doggies go
And no more with old Shep will I roam
But if dogs have a heaven
There's one thing I know
Old Shep has a wonderful home[1]

Bill actually cried as he quoted these lyrics to me.

So it was not unusual for Bill to start crying in this prayer. But just about the time he really started weeping . . . it happened. Don't tell me God doesn't have a good sense of humor. Right in the middle of Bill's prayer, that Wal-Mart commercial came on TV—the very one Bill had wanted to see all day.

I felt it in his shoulders first. I knew we had lost him. He jerked . . . kinda like a spasm. His attention was no longer

The Gaither Vocal Band

on his prayer—it was on that Wal-Mart commercial promoting his videos.

I thought, *Heaven, we have a problem!*

Bill quickly tried to wind down his prayer before the thirty-second commercial ended. So he said—IN THE MIDDLE OF THIS PRAYER, MIND YOU—"Uh, uhh, uhhhh, God bless you, bye-bye!"

Bill told God to bless Himself! Bill Gaither hung up on God! . . . for a Wal-Mart commercial!

Bill immediately quit praying, turned to stare at the TV, and started drooling. Guy, David, and I hit the floor laughing.

When the commercial was over, we wrapped our arms around each other again and finished praying. We laughed through that prayer, too. And we thanked God for laughter. I believe God smiled. God loves to hear His children laugh. What healthy father doesn't?

Laughter is a gift from God. As far as I know, none of His other creatures laugh like we do. It's unique to the human race. We also shake hands when we meet new people.

Be glad you're not a dog! They don't have hands, so they resort to other ways of greeting each other.

We all need to laugh more. Some days you may have to work at it more than others—but it's always worth the effort. Remember life is short. You're gonna be dead a long time. Laugh while you're here. Here's a toast to you (we Baptists do this with ginger ale): "May you live long and die laughing!"

> Don't try to suppress laughter.
> If you do, it will go down and spread out around your hips.
> —Steve Allen

2   Death Has No Sting

IN LATE JANUARY 2000, the Homecoming Friends were in Ireland and England for a series of concerts. Our first day in London, Bill called a rehearsal for Sunday evening at six o'clock, to be held in the basement of a local church that looked like something out of a Dickens novel. Nobody but Bill wanted to be there. The Tennessee Titans (our team) had just beaten the Indianapolis Colts (Bill's team) the previous week and were now playing St. Louis in the play-offs to see who was going to the Super Bowl. Since Bill was bitter that Indianapolis had lost and didn't care about the Tennessee–St. Louis game, he called a rehearsal. So we had to go.

The basement was musty. Old wooden foldout chairs were arranged in a semicircle. Rob Lanahan had set up a small sound system so we could hear the accompaniment tracks, and Bill stood in front of a blackboard and scratched out lyrics when we needed them. Meanwhile, Jeff Easter was on the phone every few minutes to check the score of the game.

While Rex Nelon sang a really cool bass part on the old song "Just a Little While," I sat on the back row next to David Phelps. (I love hearing his pithy comments about everything that is happening around him.) We laughed when we should have been listening and tried to act like we were paying attention whenever Bill looked in our direction. Let me just say, I was not in a prayerful mood, much less expecting what was about to happen . . .

But something did happen that night that I have only experienced two other times in my life, once when I was alone and another time when I was reading Scripture with a good friend. But it happened again. In London. In a dank old basement, while David and I were cuttin' up . . . God showed up.

I hadn't asked God to do anything sensational, incredible, or even supernatural. I wasn't seeking a new spiritual experience or the latest Christian "hot flash."

God just showed up.

Suddenly, as Jessy Dixon started singing "The Night before Easter," a holy hush swept over that room. I sat up on the edge of my seat and held my breath. I couldn't take my eyes off Jessy. I was straining to hear every word of the song that I had heard so many times . . . but had never really heard.

God's Spirit filled the place. People started crying and worshiping. The words of the song were burning in my ears. It was as though I was hearing about the cross and Christ's resurrection for the first time. I felt a tidal wave of peace and joy sweeping over me.

And to think, I could've missed this for a football game.

That was around seven o'clock in the evening. At three o'clock the following morning, my telephone rang. I remember trying to find the phone in the dark, knocking it to the floor, and then once I had recovered it, hearing, "Mark, this is Sue Dodge." By the tone of her voice I could tell immediately that something was wrong.

"Rex Nelon had a heart attack," Sue continued. "The ambulance is taking him to the hospital."

My mind didn't want to accept the news. I was thinking, *But I just saw Rex downstairs a short while ago! He was telling jokes and having a great time.*

"I'll be right there," I replied. I got up and started throwing on my clothes. I felt stunned. Just then the phone rang again. It was Joy Gardner. "What are we going to do, Mark?" she asked.

"I think we need to go to the hospital," I said. "Judy [Rex's wife] needs us."

By the time we got to the lobby to catch a cab, the man behind the hotel desk called out to us.

"I'm very sorry," he said. "I have just received a call." His voice softened as we gathered closer to hear. "Your friend died a few minutes ago."

I felt as though a bomb had dropped on us. Just a few short hours ago, Rex had been singing, laughing, and praising the Lord. Now he was gone?

Our small entourage proceeded to the hospital, and we were ushered to the room where Rex was still lying on the bed. He looked as though he were asleep.

Judy was weeping when we walked in. She looked up at me and asked, "Are they sure? Are they really sure he's gone?"

"He's gone, Judy," I answered softly.

Judy sat quietly for a moment, then suddenly she threw her hands in the air and cried out, "Okay, Father. Okay. I submit to Your will. I want to thank You for ten wonderful months as Rex Nelon's wife. Lord, we had plans for twenty-five years, but I thank You for the precious time I had with him. He was the kindest man I've ever known."

For the next two hours, Judy led us in praising the Lord.

We cried together and told stories about Rex; some of the stories were funny, and we laughed out loud. We talked about what made Rex laugh. He loved it when someone bombed on stage. When I would tell a joke and no one laughed, Rex would get a kick out of it. And he'd remind me of it every time he saw me.

I've known Judy Nelon for many years. But this night I saw beyond her external features: the blonde hair and pretty smile. I saw her faith. I saw what she really believed. When she accepted the fact that Rex was gone, she immediately began to praise God. I have never heard such wisdom, words of honor for a husband, and an outpouring of faith in God coming from someone under that sort of stress. But what is in someone always comes out when they're squeezed. In Judy's life, when the pressure came, out came thankfulness, peace, love, and joy—even in the face of death.

What Gloria Gaither wrote in a song is really true:

> There's a room filled with sad ashen faces.
> Without hope death has wrapped them in gloom.
> But at the side of a saint there's rejoicing.
> For death can't be sealed in a tomb.
> For the old rugged cross made the difference
> In a life bound for heartache and defeat.
> I will praise Him forever and ever.
> For the cross made the difference in me.[1]

Twelve hours before Rex died, I was sitting by him and Judy on the flight from Ireland to London. He seemed to be in perfect health. He had just celebrated his birthday a few days earlier. We had a great time. We laughed a lot. And he was still smiling and joking that night as he and Judy entered the elevator to go to their room. It was the last time I saw him alive.

Within a few hours, we were standing in a hospital by his body, crying, laughing, telling stories, and praising God. What we were experiencing that night in a hospital room must've been what Paul was talking about when he wrote, "'O GRAVE, WHERE IS YOUR VICTORY? O DEATH, WHERE IS YOUR STING?' . . . thanks be to God, who gives us the victory through our Lord Jesus Christ" (1 Cor. 15:55–57 NASB).

The last picture I have of Rex Nelon. He died that night in London.

*I took this picture of Rex and Judy Nelon on our flight
from Ireland to London.*

3 I Love to Laugh

I REMEMBER MY FIRST GAITHER CRUISE to the Caribbean. At that time, the Gaither Vocal Band consisted of Bill Gaither, Michael English, Jim Murray, and me. I had just joined the group. This was my first cruise, and I was excited. We performed concerts at night, had seminars during the day, and stopped at wonderful ports of call—St. Thomas, St. Martin, and St. John islands. And we ate. Breakfast, brunch, lunch, midday tea, dinner, and the infamous midnight buffet. A cruise is no time to diet. The way they feed you, it's a wonder the ship stays afloat.

The only meal with assigned seating was dinner. Every night, we dressed up in our finest suits and ate at the same table with the same group of people. I ate dinner every night with Michael English, Lisa English, Tanya Goodman-Sykes, her husband, Michael, and a few others. On the last night of the cruise, we had just begun eating our salads when a sweet, elderly lady walked up to the table and started telling us how much she had enjoyed the cruise. She said, "I know I really shouldn't do this, but I just had to stop by your table and let you know how much your music has blessed me this week."

Michael English looked up from his plate and said, "Ma'am, we're trying to eat. Can't we have a moment's peace? Nobody comes to your table while you're eating and bothers you."

The lady looked as if someone knocked the wind out of her. "Oh, I'm so sorry," she said, as she turned away, embarrassed.

The blood drained out of my face. The room began to spin. I was in shock. I couldn't believe what I'd just heard. This sweet, precious lady was slinking away, her shoulders to the ground. She had been totally humiliated by a "lead singer."

I said, "Michael, I can't believe what you just did! You've got to get up right now and apologize!"

He just stared at his plate.

My eyes darted around the table. Wouldn't someone stand up and say something? They had known Michael for years. I was the new guy. I had just gotten here.

Tanya?

Lisa?

Anybody?

Won't somebody agree with me that Michael had just made a fool of himself? That he had just "bruised the tender reed," negating everything we sang all week?

Nobody moved. They just stared at their plates.

Sad, pitiful stares.

I wanted to slap the fool out of every one of them.

Condemn them all to the charred pits of hell.

Brush the dust off my shoes and get out of there!

But I was trapped on a boat, at a table with idiots. And it was too far to swim.

So I just sat there.

Trying to catch my breath.

When I first joined the Gaither Vocal Band—
Michael English, Jim Murray, and me

Just then, Michael looked up with a big grin on his face and said, "Gotcha!" Lisa burst out laughing. Tanya and Michael gave each other a high-five. And that little lady was guffawing so hard I thought she would faint. They had pulled an elaborate practical joke on me.

I love to laugh. And I love the sound of laughter, too. Most of my friends are very funny and laugh a lot. David Musselman has been one of my good friends since college. He has a great laugh. It's big, loud, and kind of hoarse. He's an easy laugh, too. He'll laugh at anything. I remember when I was taping my video *The Last Word* at the Tivoli Theater in Chattanooga, Tennessee, I made sure David was sitting on the front row. We both have put on a few pounds since college, and he could barely squeeze into his seat. But he was there. He was on camera a lot—laughing, wiping his eyes, and loosening his tie. By the time the show was over, he'd laughed his shirt right out of his pants.

I love it when laughter hits me so hard I have to bend over, grab my sides, and cough up a kidney. Laughing when you're not supposed to is the best—like at funerals and weddings. It's so much more intense when you have to hold it in. The pressure builds, your shoulders shake, and your face turns the color of cherries. I love jokes with great punch lines and stories with endings that catch you by surprise.

But I've never been good with practical jokes. They're too much work. You've got to plan, scheme, and delegate. You've got to be convincing (which is a nice way of saying you've got to be a good liar). But the main reason I don't do practical jokes is—you've got to know how far to take it. And you've got to know when to stop. How far is too far?

In 1978, I was in a van accident with Charles Hughes, David Musselman, and Dick Bernier. If you wanna know the details, watch my *This Is the Life* video, or read my book *Out of Control*. In case you don't already know, I broke eleven bones in my body—and I escaped the worst part of the crash! Our friend Charles was in a coma for eight months.

As soon as Charles was well enough to go home from the hospital, I went to visit him. His doctors told us his short-term memory would be the last thing to return. I'd never known anyone who had lost his short-term memory, and I was especially curious. So I thought I'd have a little fun with Charles. I don't know if you'd call this a practical joke or not, but here's what I did:

I asked Charles if he could remember the crusades we did before the wreck.

He said he couldn't.

"You don't remember the stadiums we filled?" I asked.

He looked at me with excited doubt. "You're kidding?"

He was beginning to buy it. So I continued. "We packed

'em in by the thousands. We even had Donny and Marie Osmond as our special guests."

"Really?" he squealed.

I was on a roll!

"Yessiree! Don't you remember the sermon you preached when you were filling in for Billy Graham while he was in the hospital getting his toes fixed? It was a world-wide broadcast from Rio de Janeiro. Everybody got saved. Even Billy Graham called from his hospital room to re-dedicate his life."

You see what I'm talking about? I blew it. I went too far. Somewhere between "getting his toes fixed" and "Rio de Janeiro," I lost him. The gig was over. My practical joke backfired. Charles knew I was making the whole thing up.

I've gotten e-mails and letters from women who receive my Internet newsletter, "reMarks." There are currently more than forty-two thousand subscribers.[1] Most of the subscribers understand the way the electronic newsletter system works, but some of my readers think I'm sending them "secret" messages. They say that God told them I'm supposed to marry them (which is surprising because He hasn't mentioned it to me!).

The letters are a little scary sometimes. I have this picture in my head of a husky, single gal pulling up in a pickup with a "What Would Jesus Do?" bumper sticker, four kids in the back, a shotgun in one hand, a Bible in the other, pointing at me and yellin', "Take a gander, kids. Here's your new Pappy! He's the one that's been writin' us!"

Here is a sampling of some of the more interesting marriage proposals I've received:

* "I normally don't do this, but God woke me up last night and told me I was to marry you, so call me."

* "I've never written a letter like this before, but God told me we're supposed to have kids, so call me."

* "If you reject me, you're rejecting God's will for your life, so call me."

* "God told me we're gonna have the prettiest children this side of Beijing, so call me."

See? Even God, every now and then, plays practical jokes. Isn't that wonderful? God does have a good sense of humor! He's told all these women I'm supposed to marry them! That's hysterical! He knows I can't do that. So He must be playing a practical joke.

Either that, or He's a Mormon!

*My friends
Dave and Debbie
Musselman*

Bad spellers of the world, untie!

—Graffiti

4 Don't Let This Throw You

THE APOSTLE PETER REMINDS ME OF MYSELF—constantly sticking his foot in his mouth, speaking and then thinking. I love that about Peter! I do the same thing. I think he had ADD, too. People like Peter and me don't purposely place our feet in our mouths; they just naturally go there. We like to think out loud, and sometimes our ideas haven't been thoroughly thought out. The result: hoof-in-mouth disease.

I find it much easier to know what I'm thinking when I hear it from myself. But sometimes thinking out loud can get a person in trouble. Especially a person like Peter or me.

For instance, Peter was on the Mount of Transfiguration with Jesus when Elijah and Moses showed up. That in itself wouldn't have been such a big deal had Elijah and Moses not been dead for more than a thousand years! That's taking the "fashionably late" thing a bit too far. But there they were, alive and well. They arrived while Peter was taking a nap (another thing Peter and I have in common). When he woke up, Peter saw Jesus in all of His glory talking to Elijah (who had just parked his fiery chariot) and Moses (who had an odd resemblance to Charlton Heston).

Now any half-wit would have had sense enough to fall on his face and cry, "Have mercy!" or something. But not Peter. Instead of falling down, trembling, and wondering what to do next, Peter saw the potential for a "Together We Build" program. Not even the glory of Christ or the vision of Elijah and Moses was enough to stifle Peter's enthusiasm. He got so excited that he forgot to think, and he blurted, "Lord, we should build three tabernacles: one for You, one for Moses, and one for Elijah." He was babbling on so much, God had to appear in a cloud and tell Peter to shut up.

God said, "This is my Son; listen to Him."

"Listen? Who me?"

See, it was hard to get support for a building program even back then.

Another time, Peter denied the Lord. And Jesus predicted he would do it. You remember—the time Peter shot off his mouth, when he should've been listening?

It's all written down in John 13 and 14. Now, there's an interesting difference between the way Jesus said some things and the way they are printed in the Bible. When Jesus spoke to His disciples, He didn't talk to them in chapters and verses. He didn't divide His thoughts and sentences into verse one, two, or three: All of that was done by the people who translated Scripture and wrote it down so Rita Allee (who really wasn't that smart but had fast fingers) could win the Bible drill at youth camp every year.

Sometimes, when you are reading the Bible, the message of a passage takes on a whole new meaning if you don't stop at the end of that chapter, but you keep reading right on into the next chapter. For instance, if you notice, Jesus didn't stop speaking between the last line of John 13 and the first line of John 14. It's still Jesus talking to the same bunch of disciples, including rambunctious Peter. Jesus kept right on going. So try this: Read the last few verses of John 13, building speed as you read; don't slow down! Keep going! Floor it, and slam right on into the first few verses of John 14; throw it into second, and now back it down, and slow to a stop. (For you NASCAR fans, just bang into something.)

If you read the passage as Eugene Peterson translates it in *The Message,* it goes like this:

> Jesus answered, "You can't now follow me where I'm going. You will follow later."
>
> "Master," said Peter, "why can't I follow you? I'll lay down my life for you!"
>
> "Really? You'll lay down your life for me? The truth is that before the rooster crows, you'll deny me three times. [DON'T STOP; KEEP GOING] Don't let this throw you! You trust in God, don't you? Trust me."

Whoa! Think about that! Jesus told Peter before his blunder that when he committed the ultimate failure—denying that he even knew who Jesus was—that Peter could still trust Christ. And then Jesus held out a carrot for Peter to run after . . . He started telling Peter about mansions the Father is preparing for all of us. Jesus told Peter about how He had to go away, but He'll come again to receive us and take us home. Peter's sin didn't take Jesus by surprise. Jesus predicted it, and He forgave Peter even before he did it.

Jesus knows we're gonna fall. He knew it before He created us. And He doesn't want our failures to throw us. He doesn't want it to trouble our hearts. Our focus shouldn't be on our failure, but on our Father. You may stumble and fall, but trust in God and don't let it throw you.

5   Enjoy Life While You Can

SITTING OUT ON MY BACK PORCH, I notice that the old sugar maple tree has finally awakened from her long winter nap. The different shades of green make a glorious canvas for the pink and white blooming dogwoods near the back of the yard. The leaves are clapping their hands as the breeze, much like God's breath, whistles through the trees . . .

(WWHHHEeeeee, let me catch my breath. There I go, waxing eloquently, trying to write like Gloria Gaither!)

Okay, let me put it this way—it sure is pretty in Nashville in the springtime. My bird feeder is the popular eating spot for all the cardinals and chickadees in the neighborhood. This is a day, as we say in Texas, that's "hard to beat."

Tomorrow it may rain, but right now, it's sunny, cloudless, and the birds are singing, "Blue skies smilin' at me." I love days like this.

As I sit here, enjoying God's creation, I'm thinkin' about Hovie Lister and Danny Gaither, both of whom have struggled with cancer. Those two old warriors have been through chemo, stem-cell transplants, radiation, and who knows what else, yet they're still smiling. They're at peace and both say, "We're just taking it one day at a time. But today, TODAY, I'm doing fine."

With Hovie and Danny in mind, I thought, @#$%^&*! Excuse me; a gnat was crawling on my leg, and I had to squish it. Like I was saying, I thought, *All of us are terminal, but some of us have had reminders.* Jake's had diabetes; most of us Homecoming singers are overweight; Bill Gaither has had an angioplasty and hair implants . . . and my feet hurt. So unless the Lord comes back, none of us are getting out of here alive. But we're not supposed to worry about it.

Whether we're having a good day or a bad one, it's still a day the Lord has made, and He said to rejoice and be glad in it. This moment in time is really all we have. So enjoy a cup of coffee on the back porch, go outside and look at the wild-flowers, and listen to the birds singing.

Think of your life as a movie. And remember: You make a movie one frame at a time.

If there were movies on the lives of Hovie and Danny, they would show some very dark days. But they would also show men whose faith has been strengthened by enduring those times of darkness, struggle, and pain.

"Consider it a sheer gift, friends, when tests and challenges come at you from all sides. You know that under pressure, your faith-life is forced into the open and shows its true colors" (James 1:2 MSG).

So smile, be happy, and take each day as it is . . .

Oh, no! I can't believe this! It's starting to sprinkle.

This is gonna ruin my day!

STINKIN' RAIN!

6 God Says No, Too

ONE OF THE FUNNIEST STORIES I've ever heard involves the Goodmans at an all-day singing in the Amish country. Kevin Spencer promotes the outdoor event each year. On the day of the concert, Kevin thought the weather looked bad, so he wanted to hurry and get the Goodmans on stage. Well, during their performance, it started sprinkling, so Vestal asked the audience to pray with her. She raised her face toward heaven, lifted her voice in prayer, and asked God to stop the rain.

I don't know if you've ever heard Vestal pray, but she walks directly into the Throne Room, announces her daughtership, reminds God of all those scriptures He wrote, and stands firmly on every promise. I've never heard anyone pray like Vestal. And God usually tells Vestal, "Yes."

But suddenly there came a gully-washin' toad-strangler. The heavens opened, and the rain came pouring down. The concert location was in a hilly part of the country. On a steep grade uphill, behind the stage, to the left, sat a large pond, a pond that had never overflowed. It was connected to a dam that had never broken.

At that moment . . . both did.

A six-foot tidal wave came crashing toward the stage. It hit the sound system, knocking over the loudspeakers. Above the confusion, with people scrambling and chairs flying, Vestal looked at the audience and said, "Good God! He said, 'NO!' Run for your lives!"

Isn't that something? Our "Good God" said, "No."

Everyone knows a good father sometimes has to say, "No." And, evidently, sometimes He shouts it.

Me, Vestal and Howard Goodman, and Gloria Gaither

Talk is cheap because supply exceeds demand.

—Author unknown

7 My Visit with Greatness

I WAS IN ASHEVILLE, NORTH CAROLINA, for a concert on April Fools' Day. While walking back to my hotel after lunch, the concert promoter passed me in his car. He slammed on the brakes and whipped his vehicle out of the traffic and over to the curb.

"Mark!" he called. "Hurry! Mrs. Graham wants to see you!"

"Mrs. Who?"

"Mrs. Graham! You know, Ruth Graham, as in Mrs. BILLY Graham! She wants you to come up to their house in Montreat."

"You've got to be kidding. April Fools, right?"

"No, really! I'm serious. Mrs. Graham would like for you to come visit her. Maury Scobee, from the Graham organization, has driven down to pick you up."

I didn't know that Ruth Graham was aware that I was even on this planet. I had met Billy Graham when the Gaither Vocal Band had sung for the Billy Graham Crusade. I determined that I wanted to shake his hand—after all, to me, Billy Graham was "the Baptist Pope." I didn't know if I'd ever get a chance to be in his presence again on this earth, so when he walked onto the crusade platform, surrounded by crusade officials and his assistants, I lunged toward Dr. Graham as if I were Lee Harvey Oswald!

For a moment, the men around Dr. Graham froze in stark terror, but Billy Graham didn't even flinch. He just extended his hand to shake mine and smiled politely. His horrified assistants relaxed when they realized, *Oh, it's just that lunatic Lowry.*

That was my fleeting brush with greatness, so imagine my surprise to discover that Mrs. Graham even knew my name, let alone wanted to see me! I told the concert promoter to give me thirty minutes, and I raced to my hotel room to shower and change clothes. You can't enter the presence of greatness wearing casual, rumpled clothes.

Thirty minutes later, Maury Scobee was sitting in a large sport-utility vehicle outside my hotel, waiting to whisk me to Montreat. On the way, Maury told me the story of how the Grahams had purchased the Montreat property years ago. Mrs. Graham had scoured the area, searching for just the right pieces of old logs and lumber to be used in their home. They have lived in that same log home throughout their ministry, raising their children there and maintaining a low-key profile in the area. How would you feel if BILLY and RUTH GRAHAM were your neighbors? I bet you'd pay them back for all those cups of sugar you borrowed!

Some of the Grahams' closest neighbors are George Beverly Shea and his wife, Karlene. Maury and I stopped at the Sheas' home first. (I thought he might want to give me some singing tips.) At the time of my visit, George Beverly Shea was ninety-one years of age, and he was still singing at the Billy Graham crusades. His deep baritone voice is known by millions of people around the world, as he has

George Beverly Shea, his wife, Karlene, and me

sung some of the greatest gospel songs ever written. He is probably the best-known gospel singer in the history of the world. More than that, however, he is one of the sweetest, humblest, kindest, and most gracious human beings I have ever met.

I had a marvelous time visiting with the Sheas. We had coffee and played some old songs on the stereo. They told me stories, and we sang together around their piano. I thought, *Mama ain't gonna believe that I'm here singing with the legendary George Beverly Shea.* I called her on the telephone, so George could speak with her. Mama wasn't home, so Mr. Shea left her a voice-mail message she would be able to save.

I said my good-byes to George and Karlene, and then it was time to move up the mountain to visit with Mrs. Graham. Dr. Graham was in Los Angeles, receiving an award from the Ronald Reagan Library. (I think they're still typing mine up.)

Maury and I were ushered into the Grahams' large log

cabin, where we were greeted by Mrs. Graham's nurse. Mrs. Graham had recently undergone hip surgery and was still recovering in a cast, resting on a couch, but that did not diminish her radiant charm. She greeted me warmly when I was introduced to her. Lying on the couch, she had been looking out a large plate-glass window through which she could see the breathtaking view of the mountains surrounding their home.

"God was showing off when He made this place," I said, nodding toward the panoramic view outside Mrs. Graham's window.

She laughed. "He sure was," she said. "And the scenic view changes every day."

Mrs. Graham was sipping a Coke float, and she kindly offered me one, too.

How could I refuse an offer like that? I said, "Sure! I'd love to have a Coke float with you." The nurse quickly made a float for me, and Mrs. Graham and I sat there sipping and talking. Mrs. Graham told me about their house, and especially the centerpiece of the home, the large fireplace in the living room. (You've probably seen pictures of Dr. Graham sitting in front of the fireplace in a rocking chair. That's the one!) It has a beautiful mantle engraved in German with the words, "A Mighty Fortress Is Our God." Mrs. Graham loves fireplaces (the more, the merrier), so there are five fireplaces in their home. Dr. Graham wanted only two, but while he was preaching in Europe, Mrs. Graham told the workers to build five fireplaces as quickly as they could!

Mrs. Graham expressed how much she enjoyed the Gaither Homecoming videos, especially the funny parts. (That made me feel good!) She said that she rewinds the tapes and plays them over and over.

I didn't know how much time I'd have to visit with Mrs.

Me with Mrs. Billy Graham

Graham, so early in our conversation, I asked her one of my favorite questions: "Do you think Jesus knew who He was when He was a baby?"

"Well, I never really thought about that, I guess," said Mrs. Graham softly, as though she were pondering the ramifications of her answer.

"My dad believes that Jesus knew who He was the second He was conceived," I told her, "but I told Dad, 'Well, then Jesus must have been faking all those diaper changes!'"

Mrs. Graham laughed and said she'd never thought about that.

We talked a lot about God and various theological questions, and Mrs. Graham didn't seem to be in any hurry to end our conversation. I've always tried to be sensitive to someone's time, especially some of the well-known people I've been privileged to meet. They are all so busy, and I appreciate their allowing me to have any time with them at all. Besides, I know that I'm a lot like the old hair-care product,

Brylcreem—"a little dab'll do ya." I didn't want to overstay my welcome.

When I met Bob Hope, he was ninety-two years old. My friend Martha Bolton had arranged for me to visit with him at his home in California. Bob Hope didn't know me from Adam, but he was so kind and engaging. It was great fun simply to be in his presence. He hummed constantly as he showed me all around his home, which was decked out with pictures of him and Lucille Ball and a bunch of other famous comedians and movie stars. At one point during my visit, Bob Hope led me into a large, walk-in vault filled with nothing but file cabinets.

"What's in all the file cabinets?" I asked.

"Jokes, man!" Bob answered. "There's money in those cabinets."

After about twenty minutes, I sang "Thanks for the Memories" for Bob, and Martha took my picture with him, then I left. Bob didn't seem ready for me to go, but like I said, I've learned not to stay too long in the presence of greatness.

When I was visiting with Mrs. Graham, I tried to do the

Me and Martha Bolton—the great comedy writer who introduced me to Bob Hope

same thing—just keep the visit short and sweet, and don't impose too much or take up too much of her time. After about thirty minutes or so, I said, "Well, Mrs. Graham, I really need to get back, and I really don't want to keep you," trying to excuse myself tactfully.

"Oh, I wish you could stay a little longer," Ruth Graham said.

"Well, I can stay as long as you want," I admitted. "But which bedroom would be mine?"

She laughed (not realizing I was serious), and we continued to talk about serious subjects and silly ones, and we laughed together. It was a wonderful afternoon, and I will never forget my wise, gracious hostess.

I was truly in the presence of greatness.

8 Hair and Old Age

I WAS REMINDED THAT I AM GETTING OLDER when Rick Dinoff, one of my best friends, told me a story about his granddaughter, Savannah. When Savannah was a mere fourteen months old, Rick taught her to lift her little hand straight up in the air when he said, "Praise the Lord!"

At first, I chuckled at his story, and then it dawned on me: My friend Rick is a grandfather! That means he's married to a grandmother! All that is bad enough, but then I realized, Rick's only a few years older than I am!

I must be getting old.

The other day, while I was drying my hair, I noticed that my hairline is receding. Now, I'm not bald yet. I'm still doing better than some of my friends, who at my age have already lost their hair. They shall remain nameless, because they think they are fooling everybody—but I know the truth. Those "hair hats" and "comb-overs" don't fool me!

Then I noticed my eyebrows. They're getting thinner, too. But as they thin, they are being replaced by long, thick, wiry appendages, similar to cat whiskers. You pluck them out before you go to bed at night, and the next morning they're back . . . with kids! Those wire-hairs multiply like rabbits. I guess if I ever do go bald, at least I can comb my eyebrows back over my forehead.

I also know that I must be getting old because I am getting up earlier these days. I never thought that would happen. I've always wondered why old people get up at the crack of dawn. What do they have to do at six in the morning? They're retired, for heaven's sake. Sleep in. But now I know why they get up so early.

Ear hair. It scratches the pillow and wakes them up. I use my electric razor on mine. The razor groans and growls like a chain saw cutting through redwoods.

One thing I've discovered about old age: It doesn't have to slow you down. My parents are good examples of that. My mother still teaches at Liberty University, and my dad still has his law practice. They go full speed ahead, even though they are really old! Their midlife crisis was fifty years ago! They should be checking out walkers, canes, nursing homes, and motorized carts, but noooooo! They called me the other day and proudly announced that they had both completed a three-week course and were now licensed to carry concealed weapons.

Here are Mom and Dad— Mom's the one with hair!

Concealed weapons!

What's this world coming to? Mama and Daddy are packin' heat! Isn't there an age limit for that? Most people their age won't even drive after dark. But my mom and dad just used their senior-citizen discount at K-Mart to purchase a couple of "Saturday Night Specials"! Mom carries hers under a shawl.

One thing is for certain: They are not letting their age get the best of them . . . and as for those "after–Thanksgiving dinner arguments," let's just say they should be much more interesting this year!

> A gentleman is a man who can play the accordion but doesn't.
> —Unknown

9 Hot Buttons

EVERYBODY HAS "BUTTONS," triggers that, when pushed, get a reaction. Learning which buttons to push and when to push them is an art. Push someone's laugh button, and they laugh; hit their cry button, and they cry. (You want to stay away from that one, if you can.) Then there's what I call the "hot button." It's the one that sparks the most passion. And it's my favorite to push!

Especially on Mama.

One day a while back, I was home for a visit, and Mama, Daddy, and I went out to eat at an Italian restaurant. I sat across the table from Mama so I could keep an eye on her while I ate my spaghetti and meatballs with a side of sausage. The food was great, but the conversation slowed way down. We were in a lull. When I saw Mama yawn behind her hand, I thought, *Poor dear, she's getting bored.*

So I said in a loud, obnoxious voice, "You know, I heard if you drink a glass of red wine every day, you'll live longer."

Mama nearly choked on her cannoli.

I continued without even taking a breath, "I read it in *USA Today*. French people drink wine and rarely have heart problems, and they're the ones who think butter is a vegetable. Besides, the apostle Paul told Timothy to drink a little wine for his stomach's sake. Ain't it wonderful how science is always proving the Bible, Mama?"

Daddy rolled his eyes.

"MARK!" Mama shushed.

Lifting my voice so people seated at surrounding tables could hear, I proclaimed, "Yessiree! One glass of red wine a day, and you'll live forever . . . *USA Today* and the Bible agree!"

Mama's neck started to splotch. "Shhh!" she said. "Someone will hear you, and you'll ruin your testimony."

Raising my tea glass, I blared, "YEP! PAUL SAID TO DRINK A LITTLE WINE!"

That did it! Mama sat straight up in her chair, looked me dead in the eyes, cleared her throat, and went to preaching. "Paul wasn't talking about wine!" she said. "He was talking about grape juice! The Book of Habakkuk says not even to look on it while it stirreth in the cup."

"Oh, Mama, Habakkuk was talking about Nyquil. It stirreth in the cup. One shot of that stuff, and it's, 'Hello, Mr. Sandman!'"

Mama sat back in her chair in a huff. Speechless. Neck splotches spreading.

I realized that I might be pressing on Mama's "hot button" a little too long, so I finally confessed. "I hate wine, Mama. It's nasty stuff. I'll just have to die of a heart attack . . . but at least I won't ruin my testimony. Would you please pass the butter?"

Mama relaxed and went back to her cannoli. She was happy again.

You may be thinking, *Why, Mark? Why do you have to push the "hot button"?*

Well, I'll tell ya. Our dinner table conversation had hit a

lull. I had to pick things up. And I'm curious. And it's fun! Mama's reactions are always good entertainment. She's passionate about what she believes. And it's my duty to challenge her. That's why God sent me to earth. Also, I love a good debate. Create a little tension . . . ask a few thought-provoking questions . . . throw in a few neck splotches, and you've got yourself a rip-roaring conversation.

Pressing those hot buttons. It's been my blessing and my curse. It's gotten me in a whole heap of trouble. And at the same time, it's given me a career.

Mama's high-school picture

The best revenge is to live long enough
to be a problem to your children.
—Unknown

10 You're Never Too Old to Chat

THE OTHER NIGHT I was on-line checking my e-mail and noticed that my mother was on-line, too. (For those of you not familiar with the Internet, some of us have "buddy lists." And my mother was on my buddy list, so her name popped up on my screen.) I sent her an instant message. She replied.

Then, unbeknownst to me, she hollered upstairs and told my dad to get on his computer. Mom told me they were headed to a birthday party for Dr. Wilmington, who was one of my theology professors at Liberty University. She asked if I could remember a story about him that she could tell at the party.

While she was asking me this, Dad's name popped up on my buddy list. I decided I was going to treat my parents to a new experience. I knew they'd never been in a chat room. They had only recently learned how to send an e-mail. So I thought I would take them on an adventure.

After a half-hour of explaining, via instant messages, how to get in a private chat room, Dad and I finally made it to chat room "LOWRY." Mom, however, took a little longer. Here's what happened:

You have just entered room "LOWRY"

MARK:	I'M TRYING TO HELLLLLLLLPPPP
DAD:	I printed the instructions and carried them into her room.
MARK:	Does she have the right program?
MARK:	Or is it an earlier version?
DAD:	I think she has an older version.
MOM:	I AM HERE!
DAD:	Beverly, can you read this?
DAD:	Mark, she is on.
MOM:	I don't see Daddy!
MARK:	Mama, I don't have any unusual memories of Dr. Wilmington, except he's a brilliant scholar!
MOM:	He's just coming in as a semicolon.
MARK:	Can you not read what Daddy is typing?
MARK:	You're kidding?
MARK:	You can't read what he's writing?
MOM:	Yes, I can read his messages but his name is ;
MARK:	I think you should ask Dr. Wilmington for me if Jesus COULD have sinned?
DAD:	Mark, can you read my messages?
MOM:	I don't have any of him, either.
MARK:	And, if not, how could He fulfill the law if it doesn't apply to Him?
MARK:	I can see your names and your messages.
MARK:	How about you, Daddy?
MOM:	I already asked him that, and he said you could call him.
DAD:	Mark, I am not the Bible scholar that Dr. Wilmington is, but the answer is No!
MARK:	Well, Daddy, you're wrong.

MOM:	If you read these in sequence, it looks like I don't have any outstanding memories of Jesus.
DAD:	No, I have never been wrong.
MARK:	Just kidding, I don't know, either.
MOM:	That is not the case.
DAD:	It sure is.
MOM:	I don't think Jesus could sin. He said He was without sin.
DAD:	Mark, are you home?
MARK:	No, I'm in Indy.
MARK:	Of course, He was without sin.
MOM:	Mark, Rob Jackson wants you to come and do a service at LU for him in chapel.
MARK:	He DID NOT sin. But, could that be because He chose not to, not because He was incapable?
MARK:	Kewl
MARK:	(that's the Internet way of spelling "cool")
MOM:	I would like for you to walk in unannounced. The kids would go wild.
MARK:	Right
DAD:	I am listening
MARK:	Anyway
MARK:	Ask him that.
MARK:	And, doesn't it make Jesus more special when you realize He was tempted JUST LIKE YOU and me?
DAD:	ABC news is doing a segment on the cloned lamb.
MOM:	Rob said that your manager quoted him a lot of money.
MARK:	Yet He never gave in to it.

MOM: What? The money?

MARK: You have never felt the FULL WEIGHT of temptation until you've said NO to it.

DAD: Isn't it amazing—we are all talking and not on the same subject?

MARK: Read what I'm saying . . .

MARK: :)

MOM: This is so funny

MARK: You gotta learn to read the Internet way.

DAD: We can't read—we are trying to outdo each other

MARK: You gotta backtrack and read all of my sentences in context.

MOM: Can I print this?

MARK: This is sort of the way different people interpret the Bible.

MARK: You can't take the Bible out of context.

MOM: I haven't laughed this hard in a long time

DAD: Your mother is laughing out loud

MARK: So am I. I promise. I'm printing this.

DAD: She is trying so hard to out-type me—she is having a laughing fit

MOM: I can't type for laughing

DAD: Mark, this has got to end up in one of your concerts

MARK: You guys haven't listened to ONE word I've typed!

DAD: Your brother Mike just called and said he and family are home.

MARK: Jesus is MORE PRECIOUS when you realize He was tempted like YOU yet He never gave in.

MARK: He was 100% human and 100% God

MOM:	Mike just called to let us know they were back
DAD:	Mark, we have heard every word you typed, and we think you are getting very deep.
MARK:	Not 95% human and 105% God
MARK:	Oh well . . .
MOM:	I think this is wonderful
MOM:	I will be so happy to get up there and know as He knows.
DAD:	He don't give up on your old parents
MARK:	You mean, Hey don't give up on your old parents?
DAD:	Your mother has not had this much fun since she was a young girl
MARK:	Kewl!

Me with Mom and Dad

Happiness is having a large, loving, caring, close-knit family in another city.

—George Burns

11 The Spitting Preacher

YEARS AGO, on a hot Sunday morning in a little country church, I performed a twenty-minute concert before the pastor got up to speak. I took a seat on the front row, where I normally sit when I am a special guest in a church. The front row is a great place to observe body language, facial expressions, and hair transplants. I noticed, however, that everybody else was sitting in the back, but it was a Baptist church, so I didn't think much about it. In this little church, the front row was just a few feet away from the pulpit. From where I was sitting, I could count the lines in the pastor's forehead.

It wasn't bad when he started, and I was really enjoying his sermon. He could really preach, but I didn't hear him finish because he did something that distracted me.

The pastor was preaching on Yeshua Hamashiach (Hebrew for "Jesus, the Messiah"), but he had a little trouble saying it. I think he had hyperactive spit glands, because the more excited he became, the harder they worked.

In the middle of his sermon, he raised his Bible in the air, slammed his fist down on the pulpit, and sprayed, "Yeshua Hamashiach is the Lord!"

It looked as if Niagara Falls had broken loose.

I couldn't believe what I was seeing. The man was spitting all over the place. I felt like I was riding a pew through a car wash. It's a wonder he didn't electrocute himself with that much water hitting the microphone. Every time he opened his mouth, he showered another section of the congregation. He was an equal-opportunity spitter, and the louder he preached, the thicker the mist.

I wanted to look away. His cascading saliva was making me feel nauseous. But I couldn't. I knew if he should happen to look at me and see me looking as if I weren't paying attention, he might not give me a good love offering, and then I wouldn't be able to eat and buy gas, so I could get to the next town and sing for another spitting preacher.

So I continued to look at him.

He was drooling like a rabid dog. Frothing at the mouth like that demon-possessed man Jesus healed in the graveyard.

The room started spinning, and I realized that I had to get out of there. But he'd only said "in closing" twice, so I knew we had twenty more minutes. I started repeating over and over to myself, *Stare at his forehead! Don't look at his mouth! Stare at his forehead! Don't look at his mouth!*

But you know me, I never listen. My eyes were drawn to the saliva puddling around his tongue, splashing over his bottom lip. Every time his lips separated, little strings as thin as fishing line would stretch, snap, and land somewhere on the pulpit.

On some syllables he actually blew bubbles. Why did I forget my umbrella again?

At this point, I'd forgotten what he was preaching about. But he hadn't. Through the flying confetti, I could see his hands flailing and hear his voice rising. The sermon had gone on so long I wondered if he'd ever run out of spit. How much of that stuff can a body produce in an hour? I tried to get my mind off the falling saliva and onto what he was saying, but then I noticed a change. The air seemed to be clearing. The floating particles were landing and fortunately none on me. His hyperactive spit glands had finally been depleted . . . and all was well. Except now his tongue was dry, and he was having trouble pronouncing his *Ss*. By the time he said, "Shall we stand and sing a song of salvation, saints?" I could barely understand him.

At the end of the service, the pastor took me to lunch. He handed me a check and asked me what I thought of his sermon—and if I had any advice for him.

I said, "I only have one word of advice, and I don't know if you'll get it."

"Try me," he said.

I said, "Okay. Here's my advice: Swallow."

This is what I'm going to wear
the next time I go to
the spitting preacher's church

I consider exercise vulgar. It makes people smell.
—Alec Thornton

12 Tribute to a Friend

WE BURIED JOHN DANIEL (J.D.) SUMNER on November 19, 1998, his seventy-fourth birthday. The funeral started at eleven o'clock in the morning and lasted until, well, I don't know how long it lasted. Eva Mae LeFevre was still talking when everyone left, so it could still be going on, for all I know!

But, it started at eleven. Hovie Lister, Jake Hess, James Blackwood, Donny Sumner, George Younce, Bill Gaither, George Richey (Tammy Wynette's husband), Tony Brown (former piano player for J. D., now the top dog at MCA Records), and I gave eulogies.

The service began with a tape of J. D. singing "God Still Lives in This Old House." It set the tone for more of a celebration than a funeral. Jim Hill sang his classic gospel song, "What a Day That Will Be." The Masters Five (consisting of James, Hovie, Jake, Bill Baize, and John Hall) sang "I'll Meet You in the Morning," The Cathedrals sang "We Shall See Jesus" and "I'm a Child of the King," Donny Sumner sang "Ship Ahoy," The Stamps sang "The Holy City," and the Gaither Vocal Band sang "The Star Spangled Banner," which the family requested.

I sat in the choir loft with all the speakers and singers. The choir loft has the best seats in the house. When you're sitting in the audience, you only get to see one man behind a pulpit. When you're in the choir, you can scan the crowd. If you get bored looking at one person, you can stare at someone else.

I got a good look at J. D.'s funeral crowd. That was an interesting bunch of characters. I looked at the back row, and there sat Elvis. I leaned over to George Younce and said, "Wasn't that nice of Elvis to show up? Is he still working at Burger King?" (For those of you who don't know, J. D. used to sing backup for the real Elvis, so a lot of Elvis impersonators loved him, and several showed up at the funeral.)

I felt right at home.

J. D. had all sorts of friends—elderly friends, young friends, professional friends, blue-collar friends, pretty friends, ugly friends, former prisoners, ex-prostitutes, vagabonds, and other interesting characters. I saw one guy J. D. had helped to get released from prison early so he could be home with his family for Christmas several years ago.

J. D. loved to help people. In fact, that was the running theme of everyone's eulogy. He was always helping the underdog. He understood what Jesus said in Matthew 25:40: "Whatever you did for one of the least of these brothers of mine, you did for me."

I continued scanning the crowd, my eyes slowly moving from one face to the next, wondering why this person or that person was there. What had J. D. done to make all these people love him enough to reschedule their day to honor him?

As I continued to daydream, I started wondering, if there had been a funeral for Jesus and I could have sat in the choir, what would I have seen? Maybe a woman who had been caught in adultery. Or a tax collector who was so short he had to climb a tree just to see Jesus. I may have smelled the stench of fish coming from a few fishermen on the front row, and I may have seen formerly blind Bartimaeus helping usher people to their seats. I'd see others who used to be crippled or lepers or demon possessed. I'd see people walking around who used to be dead, like Lazarus and Jairus's daughter; believers and non-believers, rich and poor, sitting side by side. All having two things in common—they were all sinners, and they were all friends of Jesus.

J. D. was a lot like Jesus, after all. He, too, was a friend of sinners. I don't know who would've shown up if there had been a funeral for Jesus, but I bet He wouldn't have had any more Elvis impersonators than J. D. Jesus said we would do greater things than He did! Way to go, J. D.!

When I stood behind the pulpit at the funeral to eulogize my friend, I looked out at that most interesting audience and told them about J. D. and me. I didn't really know J. D. until we started recording the Gaither videos. I'd see him across the room laughing at George Younce or whispering a joke into Jake Hess's ear or telling the whole crowd one of his tales. And I decided I had to get to know J. D. I knew there were lots of stories behind that mischievous grin.

That was my only motive for getting to know J. D. . . . to hear some funny stories. But what I got was a friend who took me on a five-year journey.

I traveled with him to Georgia once. He told me not to eat before we left, because there was a "great steakhouse" he wanted to take me to in Macon. He said it was incredible.

I asked, "What's the name of it?"

He said he couldn't remember, but it was worth the wait. So I starved all the way to Georgia. When we finally arrived, we pulled into the parking lot of the "great steakhouse"— the Western Sizzler.

Our waitress was an older lady, a grandmother. She was kind and helpful. She brought us plenty of sweet tea and made sure there was enough ketchup for J. D.'s steak. She told us about her family and showed us pictures of her grandchildren. At the end of the meal, she brought the check. J. D. pulled a wad of cash out of his pocket and started to reach for the bill. (J. D. always carried a big roll of cash in his pocket.) The waitress and I were in the middle of a conversation. She mentioned that she had cancer and was working for just as long as she could. J. D. overheard our conversation and dropped the whole wad of cash on her tray.

Instantly.

Without thinking or taking the time to wonder if she told this same story to everybody she waited on at this restaurant.

J. D. heard "cancer," and *BOOM!* The whole wad of cash fell from his hand.

Later, I asked J. D. if he knew how much money he had given the lady. He said in that deep, booming voice, "No. And it doesn't matter."

One time we were eating at Luby's Cafeteria. J. D. was talking, and I was daydreaming. He was in the middle of one of his stories, and my attention deficit disorder kicked in. I could see his lips moving. I saw his mouth fall open as he lunged forward and laughed at himself.

But I wasn't listening. I was daydreaming.

I was thinking about how much I was gonna miss him when he died. I'd miss hearing that booming "Hello!" every time he answered the phone. I'd miss his stories. I'd miss our talks about the great mysteries of life and watching him mull them over in his mind, boil them down, and then wrap them in an eighth-grade vocabulary that everybody could understand.

He was still talking . . . and I was still daydreaming . . .

I'd miss hearing him, at the end of every song, slide down the scale an octave lower than the bass part required.

I'd miss these free lunches.

He was still talking . . .

Suddenly, I interrupted his story and blurted, "I hope you never die!"

He looked startled. My cover was blown! He knew I wasn't listening to one word he was saying. He started laughing, leaned forward, looked me straight in the eyes, and said in a deep voice that bellowed across the cafeteria, "I'll dance on your grave nine years after you're gone!"

That was the only time J. D. Sumner ever lied to me.

He did die. He never did "dance" on my grave. He didn't keep his promise. So I prayed and asked the Lord three things: to get him back for me, to make him a tenor in heaven, and to make sure there's an organ playing when he arrives. (J. D. hated organ music.)

A few days following J. D.'s funeral, the Gaither Vocal Band and the Homecoming Friends performed a concert in Lakeland, Florida. During the program in Lakeland, Bill Gaither was telling the audience of J. D.'s passing and his funeral. Suddenly, right in the middle of Bill's eloquent effort at an impromptu, onstage eulogy, something strange happened. A loud, deep, bass rumble went through the sound system. It only happened once that night. It sounded like J. D. hitting a low note.

Everybody heard it, and everybody thought the same thing . . . *J. D. has shown up!* The Bible does say we're surrounded by a "cloud of witnesses," so I'm not going to rule out the possibility of a J. D. sighting.

I hope you've heard the final project recorded by J. D. and The Stamps. The last words he ever put down on tape were these, "If I can help somebody as I pass along, then my living will not be in vain."

Thanks, J. D.; thanks for passing my way.

Me and my buddy
J. D. Sumner

We can't all be heroes because
somebody has to sit on the curb and clap as they go by.
—Will Rogers (1879–1935)

13 Letter to a Newborn Baby

HEY, KID! WAKE UP! What are you gonna do—sleep your life away? Oh, go ahead and sleep. You'll have the rest of your life to be awake.

Welcome to the wonderful world of awe!

You have started a fascinating journey. Keep your arms and legs inside the stroller and your eyes wide open because you don't want to miss a thing. Right now you're in awe of everything. As you grow older, you'll forget. Don't ever forget. Stay in awe. It's a wonderful place to live, The Land of Awe. So go on and stare for hours at a light. And who cares if you spend your first few months staring, crying, and messing your britches? To some adults all that seems like such a waste of time. But isn't a light interesting? And what's wrong with crying being your only way of communicating? It worked for Tammy Faye. And messing your britches isn't something to be ashamed of. We've all done it. Some of us just have better cologne.

You'll hear a lot of things while you're living in your parents' home. Your mother will probably try to get you to clean your plate because there are starving kids in India.

Well, cleaning your plate isn't going to help them. Don't let her fool you. She's only saying that because her mother told her that. And her mother before her.

And Eve probably told that one to Cain and Abel. Go ahead and clean your plate, but do it because you're grateful, not because you don't want anyone in some foreign country to get it.

Realize you are rich. We all are. Rich in the things that matter. Eating that last meatball on your plate doesn't really matter. Kindness matters, generosity matters, and sacrificial love matters.

Life is short. It really will be over before you know it. So live while you're here, 'cause you're gonna be dead a long time.

Looks are not important. They will seem important when you're a teenager. But when you go to your twentieth high-school reunion, you'll see that looks don't last. Gravity is the great equalizer.

Your mom and dad love you a lot, so when you become a teenager, go easy on 'em. This is the first time they've ever been parents. And someday, when you become a parent, go easy on your kids. Because they get to pick your nursing home.

God's mercies are new every morning, and it's a good thing, because you'll wear them out every day.

Always remember, i before e except after c.

When you're out of money, you can't just write a check.

Turn the lights out when you leave a room.

Become potty trained as soon as possible. You don't know it now, but you're really making a mess, and people don't really enjoy cleaning up after you.

Ask Jesus into your heart as soon as you understand what He did for you.

And remember, everything you see was created by a

word from God. Except you. When you look at stars in the sky, remember, they were created by a word from God. When you look at an eagle in flight, remember, it was created by a word from God. When you look at mountains, remember, they were created by a word from God. But, when you look in the mirror, don't ever forget, you were created by the very hand of God . . . in His very image.

Your parents helped out a little.

JUST IN CASE YOU FORGOT

- If God had a refrigerator, your picture would be on it.

- If God had a wallet, your photo would be in it.

- He sends you flowers every spring and a sunrise every morning.

- When you want to talk, He'll listen.

- He could live anywhere in the universe and yet He chose your heart.

- And that Christmas gift He sent you in Bethlehem?

Face it, friend, He's crazy about you!

—Author unknown

14 Mediocrity Is Its Own Reward

I SAW MY FRESHMAN HIGH-SCHOOL PICTURE the other day, and I looked scarrrrry! I had a bad case of acne when I was a kid. On top of that, I was really skinny, with a big head (I took up two spaces in the yearbook), a "proud-as-a-peacock" grin, and braces. What can I say? I was a hunk!

I looked like a "before" picture for Clearasil. But I had a good personality, so that made up for my looks. Or so I told myself.

My older brother, Mike, was good-looking, athletic, and the star basketball player at our school. (It was a private Christian school with only twenty students. I was the only one in the school who wasn't on the team, which made doing "the wave" in the stands a little difficult.)

Now my brother is forty-four years of age. He doesn't get around like he used to. He's aging. He's got four kids. One of them is a teenager. His hairline is receding and turning gray. And his pecs aren't perky anymore. They're sagging like the rest of him.

There's something to be said about being average-looking all your life. You got nothing to lose. You only "ripen" with age like the hidden grape that's overshadowed by the more "visible" grapes on the vine. You may not have been elected homecoming queen or voted "Most Handsome," but you have finally come into your own. You now pity those poor, narcissistic colleagues whom people used to call "pretty," the so-called beautiful people. But as *we* age, *we* only get better . . . not always so with the pretty people. They panic. Have you noticed? They speak often about their lost youth. They need constant reassurance that they still look as good as they did in high school.

Oh, we tell them they look as lovely as they did in elementary school, if they need to hear it. Don't we? But deep inside, we're smiling. "Oh, you look exactly the same," we tell them. "Those crow's-feet around your eyes and extra chins around your neck are hardly noticeable . . . from fifty feet!" I don't really call this lying. I call it salvaging a shattered ego. Mercy with a bit of flattery. Time has done a lot more damage to them than it has to us. The walls are cracking, the roof is leaking, the plumbing needs repair, and more bad weather is on the horizon. This life is short and full of trouble. And the advance of Father Time has left its trail.

I was switching channels the other day, going from the Game Network to CNN when I stumbled upon the Operation Channel. I'd never noticed it before. It's way up in the 800s somewhere, hidden between the Trailer Trash Shopping Network and C-Span. I wasn't expecting it, and I nearly threw up when I saw what they were airing. They were performing a face-lift on a lady. But I didn't know it was a lady at first. All I could see was a bloody skull with what looked like flesh-colored vinyl couch covers stretched by a doctor's pliers. I could hear the doctor talking in a monotone voice, explaining every stitch, stretch, and staple. He put collagen in her lips to make them more voluptuous. He popped fat bubbles in her eyelids to remove the bags. He took a laser gun and blasted the top layer of skin to smooth out wrinkles (which made her look like a burn victim).

He took her whole face off. It looked very painful.

I don't know why I thought it, but I did. I was standing there, and the only thing that kept me from hurling my Big Mac and supersize fries was an incredible marketing idea that popped into my head: *Wouldn't it be cool if you could do that at home?* Instead of Tupperware parties, you could throw face-lift parties and invite all your vain friends.

I've got a couple of narcissists in my corral of friends.

In fact, one of 'em just had a complete overhaul . . . face-lift and everything. I told him to make sure he didn't come out looking like a sock monkey. Have you seen those little old ladies in south Florida who have spent too much time under the plastic surgeon's scalpel? Their faces are so tight that the corners of their mouths are at their earlobes. They look like the sock monkeys I used to play with when I was a kid. If you are a plastic surgeon, you can make a killing in Florida.

I'm not saying you should or shouldn't have plastic surgery. I say, if something's sagging . . . tack it. But if you do get plastic surgery, just make sure they don't take off more years than your hands will allow . . . because your hands will tell on you. You can't get a hand-lift. (I don't think.) It doesn't matter how tight they get the face, the hands never lie.

I watched a well-known comedienne on Larry King talking about her numerous plastic surgeries. I was fascinated. I've always liked her. And I thought they had done a good job on her face. In fact, she looked so young she said her age was "a secret." A few minutes later, she lifted her right hand to lightly brush the hair out of her eyes. I moved closer to the screen. "What is that?" It looked like the creature from the black lagoon rising . . . swollen, gnarled knuckles . . . crooked fingers . . . age spots the size of quarters.

Her secret was out.

So let the former pretty people fight to regain their former looks. I, personally, have no desire to go back. Braces and acne were my lot. And, young people, don't let the "pretty people" make you feel you can't succeed. I've heard it said it's the A student who ends up teaching; it's the C student who owns the company. And like I've always said, it's the dull knife that butters the bread. So hold your head high, throw your shoulders back, stand tall, and be glad you're average. Remember, as my good friend Jean Giraudoux always says, "Only the mediocre are always at their best."

Several years ago I was reading the Sunday paper and saw a three-stanza poem that I wish I had written. I think it says it best:

Kids Who Are Different

Here's to the kids who are different,
The kids who don't always get A's,
The kids who have ears twice the size of their peers,
And noses that go on for days.

Here's to the kids who are different,
The kids they call crazy or dumb,
The kids who don't fit, with the guts and the grit,
Who dance to a different drum.

Here's to the kids who are different,
The kids with the mischievous streak,
For when they have grown, as history's shown,
It's their difference that makes them unique.[1]

I stole the seal!

When I go to the beauty parlor, I always use the emergency entrance. Sometimes I just go for an estimate.
—Phyllis Diller

15 Missed the Boat

MY FRIEND RICH MULLINS was killed in a car wreck on September 19, 1997. Rich was a songwriter and contemporary Christian music artist, perhaps best known for his song, "[Our God Is] An Awesome God."

My most memorable time with Rich was on a Sandi Patty "Inspirational" cruise. Sandi had invited Kathy Troccoli, Rich Mullins, Max Lucado, and me to help provide the "inspiration" for the cruise.

When we arrived in St. Martin, I talked Rich and two of our friends into riding scooters. The four of us grabbed a taxi, and I told the driver to take us to a scooter rental company. We talked all the way, and nobody paid attention to how we got to this particular scooter company.

We jumped out of the cab, threw down a credit card, and took off on the mopeds. We had only a few hours in St. Martin, so we had to do all of this quickly. When it came time to return the scooters and head back to the ship, we couldn't find the scooter company! We looked at the map we'd been given. It made no sense. We circled the island several times. We stopped and asked directions from people who couldn't help us. We were totally, absolutely, hopelessly lost. And it's not that big of an island!

We should have just gone back to the ship, given the keys to someone, and asked him to return the scooters for us. Or maybe we could have called the owner and told him where we'd left them. It would have been much less expensive than the price we paid.

We missed the ship . . . which departed St. Martin on time and was scheduled to be at sea the next day headed for Nassau. We had to spend the night in St. Martin, fly to San Juan and spend the night, then fly to Miami to catch another flight to Nassau to meet the ship. None of us had a change of clothing . . . we hadn't expected to miss the ship in the first place! Nobody had passports . . . they were back on the ship with our clothes. No toothbrush. No shampoo. No clean underwear. We had nothing but the clothes on our backs.

I had to smooth-talk our way in and out of customs, leaving San Juan, entering the U.S., leaving the U.S., and entering the Bahamas. How did I do? Fine, thank you. I got us all to the ship without going to prison. (The handcuffs were just for show.)

I was embarrassed, though. I am rarely late to anything, much less miss an event altogether. Although she had to cover two days without two of her featured artists, Sandi forgave us.

When Rich Mullins died, I was shocked. His death hit me hard. I went to Rich's wake, where I saw a lot of mutual friends, many of whom had known Rich from the early eighties. I loved hearing their stories about him. I told my story to a woman who had known Rich the longest. She laughed and told me that missing the ship wasn't my fault. Stuff like that happened to Rich all the time. He'd be halfway around the world when he'd realize he didn't have his passport. He was always losing his car keys or locking them in the car. He really was an absent-minded genius.

When I heard Rich had died in a car wreck, the first thing that went through my mind was, "No! I'm not through with him yet!" I wanted to spend more time with him. I wanted to explore his mind a little more. He knew things about grace that I am just beginning to understand. He truly walked humbly with God. He may have missed the boat, but I know he didn't miss heaven.

> The race is not always to the swift,
> Nor the battle to the strong,
> Nor satisfaction to the wise,
> Nor riches to the smart,
> Nor grace to the learned.
> Sooner or later bad luck hits us all.
> No one can predict misfortune.
> Like fish caught in a cruel net or birds in a trap,
> So men and women are caught
> By accidents evil and sudden."
> (Eccles. 9:11–12 MSG)

Sandi Patty and me singing on my Mark Lowry on Broadway video

*Doing my "Sandi Patty"
impersonation*

16 How I Weaseled My Way into the Gaither Vocal Band

BACK IN 1980 (Lord, I'm starting to sound like my grandfather), when I graduated from Liberty University, I started traveling and singing concerts in churches. Roy Morgan, who also graduated that year, called me and said he wanted to start a booking agency; specifically, he wanted to book me. I said, "Sure, I ain't got no bookin's!" So Roy took the Baptist Bible Fellowship church directory and started calling pastors. Very few of these preachers knew who I was, but Roy was a pretty good salesman, and he talked a number of them into scheduling me.

I traveled to concerts in a car crammed full with records in the back and my clothes on one of those bars that stretched across the backseat.

When I first started out, I would always use the church's sound system. But most of those small Baptist churches had little old men with hearing aids in both ears who also worked on the buses (I mean, a knob is a knob) running those sound systems. All of my soundtracks were on individual cassettes (one song per cassette), and it would take them *forever* to change those tracks. And when you're standing in front of hundreds of people waiting for the next song to start, those few seconds can feel like an eternity. So I eventually bought a BOSE sound system that fit in the trunk of my car.

When I got to the church, I would set up the sound system and put the BOSE mixer/amp and cassette tape deck on the Lord's Supper table. (I stood by the Lord's Supper table and sang while running my own sound.) Then I'd go set up the record table in the lobby.

I traveled across the country, stopping every two hundred miles to sing in one Independent Baptist church after another, whether they remembered they'd invited me or not. I sang in Baptist churches primarily because that's the denomination I was raised in, and they were the only people who remotely knew who I was. I sang for youth rallies, revival services, camp meetings, anywhere Roy got someone to allow me to set up my system and sing. (I think I even hit a few Waffle Houses by mistake.)

I remember thinking, *If I could just get a chance to sing in a Southern Baptist church, I would really make it!* (I'd heard their love offerings were better.) But Independent Baptists (us) thought Southern Baptists (them) were liberal. Why? Because they had a COOPERATIVE PROGRAM!!! (Wooooooooo, scaaarrrrrry!) And our preachers preached long and hard against it! There had to be some reason we weren't Southern Baptists—after all, we were Baptists and definitely Southern. So, I guess that was the culprit—the "cooperative program." To this day, I'm still not sure what the cooperative program is, and I'm not really clear on what is so bad about it (although I'm sure some of my Independent Baptist friends will now be happy to inform me). But whatever it is, it separated the two groups.

One day I was invited to perform for a Southern Baptist

youth event, and after that, I got to sing in more Southern Baptist churches. I found Southern Baptists to be really nice people, not nearly as evil as I'd heard. I liked them . . . and they liked me!

In the meantime, Roy Morgan had started promoting concerts. He promoted some Gaither shows, and he talked to Bill about having me on one of their programs. I was hanging pictures in my house in Acworth, Georgia (a suburb of Atlanta), when Roy called me and said that Bill Gaither was interested in talking to me.

My heart skipped a beat. I knew Bill Gaither had a comedy team, Hicks and Cohagen. I thought that maybe they were leaving, and he was looking for a new opening act. But as quickly as my heart had jumped, it came crashing down. Bill wasn't looking for a new opening act; he was looking for a baritone.

Ugh! A baritone!

Gary McSpadden, who had been in the Vocal Band for twelve years, left the group. (Nowadays, I tell everybody that Bill was looking for somebody as good-lookin' as Gary, and I was the obvious choice. But, that's not altogether true. It's true, but not altogether. It's all in how you define the word *true*.)

Anyway, Bill was looking for a baritone. The sound of it— *baritone*—sounded soooooo boring! I had never sung baritone. I usually sang lead, and I didn't really know what baritone was. Quartets (which I had never much liked, much less sung with) have baritones. And that's what Bill Gaither was asking me to do—sing baritone. I knew I couldn't hear the part, so I called a friend over who had a good "ear" and could hear parts extremely well. I bought the Gaither Vocal Band's CD that included "Daystar," the song Bill had asked me to learn for the audition. My buddy sang the baritone part in my ear. I memorized it, then I headed for Nashville.

My brother went with me. I knew I wouldn't get the job. I knew once Bill heard me try to blend, swell, and harmonize (which is what quartets have to do), he would say, "Thanks. Don't call us; we'll call you. But if you'd like to buy one of my new videos since you're already here . . ." But I went to Nashville for the audition anyway! After all, I had been invited, and I wanted to meet Bill Gaither.

When we got to the little studio in Nashville, Bill Gaither, Michael English, and Jim Murray were already there. I walked in, met them all, and we went to the microphones and proceeded to sing "Daystar." There I was—the guy they wouldn't let in "The Sounds of Liberty" (a traveling ensemble in college), and now I was standing next to Bill Gaither, Michael English, and Jim Murray, singing "Daystar."

I approached the audition nonchalantly. I was a bit amused. I wasn't really nervous, because I knew I wasn't going to get the job. I just wanted to meet Bill Gaither and make him laugh. I knew if I made him laugh, he'd never forget me. So I made it my goal, not to get the job, but to make Bill laugh. And I did.

It took awhile, but I won Michael and Jimmy over, too. It took a little longer for Michael than it did Jimmy. I often wondered why Michael took so long to warm up to me. I'm really harmless, for the most part. So years later, after we had become good friends, I asked him. Michael said, "Well, I'd just never met anyone who, on the first trip with the Gaithers, would take their socks and shoes off, stick their feet up on the kitchen table, and clip their toenails."

Honestly, I have no recollection of that. I did it at Ruth Graham's house, but I don't remember doing it on the Gaither Vocal Band bus.

After the audition in Nashville, Bill asked me to go on the road with them and see how well we worked together in concert. My first concert with the Gaither Vocal Band was in a church in Knoxville, Tennessee. Bill had told me what songs to learn. I listened to the tapes, studied the songs, and called my friend over to help me figure out the parts. Then I hit the road with the Gaither Vocal Band.

That first night, Bill chose a song that he had not warned me to learn. It was called "Cancelled, Worthy." The first time I heard that song I was walking to the front of the stage to sing it! And that's the truth! I just mouthed "watermelon, applesauce, watermelon, applesauce . . ." No one knew the difference because all the other singers were singing the correct words.

I toured with the GVB, still auditioning, for a couple of months. At Praise Gathering 1988, Bill asked me to join the group. I'm now working on my second decade with them. I'm still traveling with the Gaithers, but the toenail clippers are at the house.

And that's how I weaseled my way into the Gaither Vocal Band.

> We aren't worried about posterity;
> we want it to sound good right now.
> —Duke Ellington (1899–1974)

17 Grumbling or Grateful

WHEN I FIRST STARTED TRAVELING AND SINGING, I met a lot of other singers who were also in the fledgling stages of their careers. Almost all of the Christian music artists had a story of a church that didn't pay them enough. I never had any of those sad tales—except that one church in Pittsburgh that didn't give me a dime. I have never forgotten that church. But I got a good story out of that one. I put it on my *This Is the Life* video . . . and made a killing! So maybe they paid me, after all!

Sometimes, while listening to my colleagues grumble, I'd think, *Y'all are bitter. What's the big deal? All because you didn't get enough money in the love offering? Maybe if you'd been a little more lovable, there would have been a little more "love" in the offering.*

But don't think that I am immune from the grumbling "virus." I catch myself grumbling now and then. Usually, I grumble over things such as having to pack again, catching another plane, going out on my three-day workweek, or going on a cruise . . .

CAN YOU BELIEVE THAT?

I actually complained about going on a cruise! Where you eat great food thirteen times a day! Where they leave a little chocolate mint on your pillow at night! Where you're waited on hand and foot! Where the Caribbean sun caresses your body! Where the beaches are breathtaking! Yes, I complained about having to go on a cruise.

You know you're spoiled when you gripe about cruises.

While people were shoveling their grandmothers out of snow heaps in Iowa, I said, "Oh, no! Not another cruise!"

Actually, I've been on a lot of cruises. I really enjoyed the first few hundred cruises. But then I realized you can't get off those ships just anywhere if you decide to pull over for some fast food between one of the thirteen meals a day. Until they decide to stop, you're stuck. But that's no reason to grumble.

I grumbled, and I'd like to privately confess it to you at this time.

Don't you know that God hates grumbling? Listen! First Corinthians 10:10 says, *"Do not grumble,* as some of them did—and were *killed* by the destroying angel"* (NASB; emphasis added).

Whew! God doesn't like grumbling.

Israel watched God part the Red Sea. When they got thirsty, He gave them water from a rock. When they got hungry, He provided manna from heaven. When they got tired of manna, He sent them quail.

Yet they grumbled about the food. They grumbled about the desert. They grumbled about Moses and Aaron.

Can't you hear the Lord now? "I give . . . I give . . . I give . . . and all you do is complain!"

I'm so glad we don't live in Old Testament times. Do you remember what happened back then, when God got a bellyful of His children grumbling? Yep, He killed 'em.

That's one serious "time-out"!

They got touched by an angel, and it wasn't the sweet Roma Downey or Della Reese–type, either! God used one of those big Arnold-Schwarzenegger-terminator-type angels to punish them for their grumbling.

When do I grumble?

I grumble when I'm not grateful, which is really silly of me, since I've got a lot to be grateful for. Grateful for life, a full stomach, and a roof over my head. Grateful for the sun, moon, and stars, the snow on the grass, and the eyes to see it all. Grateful to be loved and forgiven by a merciful Savior.

Lately, I've discovered something: When I'm truly grateful . . . I don't mind cruises so much.

Me and Mama—dueling chins

18 Recording Nightmares

WHEN I FINALLY DECIDED to record *But Seriously,* my all-singing project, it was strictly because my mother made me. I hadn't recorded a solo project in many years. I just didn't have any great desire to record again. But Mama had been harping on me for years to do another one, and you know mamas. They all think their kid can sing. I told her she better be ready to buy a lot of 'em. And she has. I bill her every month. I give her a 2-percent discount. After all, she is my mother.

But I had no desire to record an all-singing project, mainly because it's such a struggle. You might be thinking, *What kind of struggle? What pain? You get to record in million-dollar studios and sing on million-dollar microphones and have million-dollar producers who make you sound like two cents. What kind of struggle could it be?*

Well, I'll tell ya.

First of all, I have to concentrate for long periods of time—sometimes thirty to forty minutes in a row! For me, that is difficult work. Besides that, I have to sing lines over and over and over and over, until I get them right!

When I'm in the studio with the headphones on, with

the reverb turned up just right, and I'm singing through a million-dollar microphone, I tell you, I sound like Michael Bolton. Then I go into the control room, listen to it back, and I sound like Jerry Lewis.

When I'm recording my vocals, the producer will listen to me sing a line, stop the tape, and push the little button that allows me to hear what he's saying and allows him to act like it's a scepter. With feigned sincerity, he says, "That's good, Mark, but you were a little flat; let's get on pitch, please."

So I try singing while raising my eyebrows to help me get on pitch. I always raise my eyebrows when I'm trying to get on pitch.

The tape stops.

"That's good, Mark, but you need to give me more passion, please."

I sing it again. This time, I'm trying to sing it with passion.

The tape stops.

"That's good, Mark, now give me just a little more presence" (whatever that means).

I sing it again.

The tape stops.

"That's good, Mark, but you need to get in the pocket."

At this point I throw the headphones on the floor, storm in the control room, and say, "Pitch? Passion? Presence? Pocket? PICK ONE! I can't do everything at once."

When the recording is finished, it's like after the baby's born. The birth pains are over, and I've got a CD copy sitting in my CD player. It is the best record I've ever made, thanks to Michael Sykes and Lynn Keesecker, my producers, who still haven't told me if I ever did give them any presence.

Oh, and I better thank Mama. So, thanks, Mama. And be sure to get that check in the mail soon.

19 Grow Where You're Planted

I LOVE PONDERING THINGS. I enjoy getting with friends and discussing deep, theological, and complex ideas. Of all the questions I've been asked in my life, the one that I have the most trouble answering is, "How do I get started in Christian music?"

I'm not sure.

I get asked this question by a lot of young people who look at me as if their future lies in my answer. They think that since I sing with Bill Gaither, I've made it. I must tell you, I feel the same. But I have no idea how *you* can sing with Bill Gaither. I can tell you the events that happened in my life and brought me to the place where Bill asked me to join the group, but I never planned it. I never thought it out. It was not a goal of mine. But, boy, is it fun!

The Gaither Vocal Band is the first group I've ever sung with. (Except for the little trio I had when I was a kid in Houston. I called us "The Mark Lowry Trio." It included me, Mama, and the preacher's daughter, Christy Clayton. I always sang the lead, and Mama and Christy had to sing the parts. We thought we were The Singing Rambos.)

So when Bill asked me to join the Gaither Vocal Band, I was surprised, because I had never sung baritone. You'd think to join a VOCAL band you would at least have to know how to sing your part. But you don't. Bill can teach you. He will sing it really loud in your ear until you get it. At least, that's my experience.

If you asked one hundred Christian artists how they got to where they are today, you'd get one hundred different answers. There's really no secret to making it in Christian music. You don't go to college, study music, graduate, and join "Take 6." (You gotta go to summer school for that.)

But, for all those who have asked, "How can I get started in Christian music?" and for all those in the future who may ask, here is my last word on the subject.

Grow Where You're Planted

In other words, sing where you are. Sing all the time. Sing in the shower. Sing in the car. Join the choir. Sing at nursing homes, youth retreats, weddings, funerals, bar mitzvahs, and at the openings of envelopes. In other words, sing anywhere, anytime, for any reason.

So often I talk with aspiring Christian musicians who say, "I just want to minister with my music."

"Where are you ministering with your music right now?" I ask.

They look back at me as though I had hit them with a flying tortilla. The expression on their face says, *The audacity of you to ask such a thing!*

"Well, I'm not really ministering anywhere right now. I'm just sorta letting my light shine for Jesus and waiting until I get a record deal."

Great! Shine all you want. But if you really want to minister through music, get started right where you are. You don't need your name up in lights to sing. All sorts of opportunities are right in front of you if you will open your eyes and grow where you are planted. I'm learning that if I want God to allow me to do "big" things, I must be faithful in the "little" things. Otherwise, He won't trust me with the big things.

Build a Fire

"If you build it, they will come." Make people want to hear you sing. Rehearse. Practice. Take voice lessons. And when you do perform, make it look easy. Even if you feel that one, lonely sweat droplet running down your back, don't ever look nervous. The easier you make it look, the more the audience will relax and enjoy the music and message.

"How do you make it look easy?" I hear you asking.

Practice. Practice. Practice.

The Six "P's"

Pitch, Pocket, Presence, Passion, Plan, and Perseverance.

Pitch: If you can't sing on pitch, learn to type.

Pocket: Ride the rhythm. If you can't do that, you can always preach.

Presence: This is "magnetism" on stage. Some people call it "charisma," but since I'm a Baptist, I have to refer to it as "presence." People notice the person with presence. They walk in a room and their presence commands attention. (Vestal Goodman has this.) It's hard to describe, and I really don't think you can teach it. You either have it or you don't.

Passion: Whatever vocation you choose in life, it should be something you are passionate about. It's a lot more fun than singing something you don't really believe. You should never sing a song you are not passionate about, because it will show. Before you select a song, read through the words, know what it's saying, make sure you believe it, and get passionate about it. If you're bored, know this: The audience is bored, too.

Plan: Know where you're going. Have it all mapped out on paper or in your head. You may not know how the evening will end, but you should definitely know how it will start. Make sure you've practiced and are as prepared as possible, mentally, physically, and spiritually.

Perseverance: Don't quit. Sing. Don't quit. Laugh at your critics. Don't quit. Run from negative people. Don't quit. Shoot for the stars . . . you may hit the moon! But whatever you do, don't ever . . . ever . . . quit.

Keep It in Perspective

Right before you go onstage, take a few deep breaths. Forget about yourself. Give the performance to God, then go out and do your best. This is not a competition. You have already won the prize—Christ Jesus. And one hundred years from tonight, nobody's gonna remember what you sang anyway. Most of them won't remember by the next day.

Wayne Watson told me one time, "One great night won't make you, and one bad night won't break you." Wayne's right. So just relax; the One you're singing for loves to hear all His children sing, good singers or bad, Sandi Patty or Brother Worley. (Every church has a Brother Worley. He knew how to pray, but his singing could split a church . . . and an eardrum.)

Another thing you can do to improve your skills is to attend some of the Christian music seminars that are available. For example, as a fledgling songwriter, I attended the

Christian Artists Music Seminar. This is where I learned how to write lyrics. Each seminar is led by a successful songwriter. I learned about meter, rhyme, hooks, and all the other "tools" I needed to craft great lyrics. Also, there are competitions for songwriters, soloists, groups, actors, dancers, and much more.

The Gospel Music Association also conducts a music seminar each year, and that, too, is a great opportunity to learn from people who have been successful in Christian music. For those who love gospel music, let me recommend Ben Speer's Stamps/Baxter School of Music. Bill Gaither attended it when he was a kid. It's a great school for learning parts, harmony, shaped-notes, and the ins and outs of gospel music.

So, how do you get started in Christian music?

I'm really not sure.

But if you truly have talent and a desire to get into Christian music, God will make a way for you to use the gift He has given you.

If not, you can always type.

> Little-known fact: Elvis Presley was not chosen for his high-school glee club because the director said Elvis couldn't sing well enough.

20 Simply Indispensable

WHENEVER I GET TIRED AND WEARY, I sometimes try to think what I would do if I ever quit traveling and performing. I don't know how to do anything else besides sing and tell stories. If I weren't doing that, I guess I'd be somewhere, saying, "You wanna supersize that?"

I'm so fortunate to be a part of the Gaither Homecoming phenomenon. After you've observed several Gaither concerts, you might notice that everyone on our stage is essential, but no one is indispensable. These concerts are not about any single artist or group of artists. It's not a Happy Goodman happening or a Gaither Vocal Band show or a Jake Hess concert.

The Gaither Homecoming Family is a group of people coming together to sing about something they all really believe. It's a bunch of beggars telling other beggars where they found some food. This bunch just does it in harmony.

It's a snapshot of the body of Christ.

I've heard my father say, "If someone wants to know how indispensable he is, he needs to get a glass of water, stick his finger in it, pull it out, and see how big a hole he leaves." I've never forgotten that. And I remind myself of it often.

It's so good to know that God and His plan aren't riding on my back—or anyone else's, for that matter. It's riding on His. When I was in college, a big debate raged in one of our classes. The debate was, "Has the church of Jesus Christ failed in the twentieth century?"

I said, "Of course not. Jesus said, 'On this rock I will build my church, and the gates of hell will not prevail against it.' It's His church, not our church, and if it fails . . . He fails. And, that ain't gonna happen." (I was a smart aleck even in college.)

God doesn't *need* any of us; He chooses to work through us. And when Bill Gaither goes to glory, God will raise someone else up. When Billy Graham takes his flight, God will raise someone else up. And when I'm gone . . . there'll be a moment of silence. My family and friends have earned it.

Isn't it good to know that the weight of the world isn't on any of our shoulders? It's on His, and He can bear it. All we gotta do is show up, follow, and sing as loudly as we can.

> No matter how rich you become,
> how famous or powerful,
> when you die the size of your funeral
> will still pretty much depend on the weather.
>
> —Michael Pritchard

21 Hope

ONE OF THE GREATEST SINGERS ever to present a gospel song was a man whose life resonated with the message of hope. That man was Glen Payne, who sang for years with The Cathedrals. In the more than fifty years Glen sang for the Lord, he rarely missed a concert date because of sickness. He didn't even catch a cold or develop laryngitis, and for a singer, that truly is a miracle. Then in a matter of weeks, he was gone.

When we first heard the news that Glen had passed away, the Gaither Vocal Band was in Pittsburgh, Pennsylvania, singing to a sold-out crowd in the Civic Arena. Most of the sixteen thousand people in attendance had not yet learned that Glen had died, and I was wondering how Bill was going to break the sad news that one of gospel music's best had gone home.

Toward the end of the program, with all of our Homecoming Family sitting on stage, Bill walked over to Howard Goodman and rested his arm on the back of Howard's chair. "We've had a rough year," Bill said, looking at Howard but speaking to everyone in the arena. "We've lost several of our Homecoming Family . . ." Then Bill went on to tell the audience that Glen had passed away earlier that afternoon. It seemed as though everyone in the audience sighed at once.

As he spoke, Bill told how he had awakened in the middle of the night and read Psalm 91, which reminded him of a prayer that, years ago, his mother used to pray with him, Danny, and Mary Ann right before bedtime: "Five little angels around my bed. One at the foot and one at the head. One to watch, one to pray, and one to take my sins away."

Even as Bill spoke, I couldn't help but think of his brother, Danny. When Danny was undergoing the worst part of a stem-cell transplant ordeal, all alone, sick, and depressed, he recalled that little prayer his mother used to pray before bedtime. Danny opened his eyes and saw an angel walking back and forth at the foot of his bed.

One of the greatest singers of all time— Glen Payne

Danny's like me. He doesn't see angels on a regular basis. In fact, I don't think I've ever seen one. But sometimes, when we are at our lowest, our heavenly Father opens our "spiritual eyes" and lets us catch a glimpse of what's going on all around us and see a little bit of what He's up to.

Bill went on to say, "I opened the Bible that night and read Psalm 91:11: 'For he shall give his angels charge over thee, to keep thee in all thy ways'" (KJV). The passage inspired him to write a new song, which his daughter, Suzanne, helped him to finish:

Lord, Send Your Angels

When I'm alone and the light slowly fades.
Cold with the night closing in
I know the shadow of the Almighty wings
Lord, won't you send them again?

Lord, send your angels to watch over me.
I'm so afraid of the dark.
Lord, send your angels to watch over me,
Wrap me in sheltering arms.

Shield me.
Keep me.
Hold me safe in your arms.
Lord, send your angels to watch over me,
Wrap me in sheltering arms.

Sometimes the child inside of me cries
With fears of the dangers unseen
And questions with answers I can't seem to find
Then you send your angels to me.[1]

When the song had finished, there was hardly a dry eye in the arena. The next thing I knew, all the singers onstage were singing, "Heaven's home is not so far away, and we'll reach it some glad day. Heaven's home is now my final goal. There to live while ages roll. And what a happy day 'twill be. What a glorious jubilee."[2]

Scripture says that we don't grieve like those who have no hope. We who trust in Christ have a blessed hope, not just that we will see Him, but also our loved ones who have gone to heaven before us.

I love the way *The Message* says it:

> And regarding the question, friends, that has come up about what happens to those already dead and buried, we don't want you in the dark any longer. First off, you must not carry on over them like people who have nothing to look forward to, as if the grave were the last word. Since Jesus died and broke loose from the grave, God will most certainly bring back to life those who died in Jesus. (1 Thess. 4:13–14 MSG)

I've heard that passage quoted at funerals all my life, but on that Friday night in Pittsburgh, I watched thousands of people live it out, on their feet singing, some with their hands raised in the air, many with their eyes closed, grieving, yet full of hope. They weren't just quoting a verse or singing a song; they were experiencing the truth of the message.

At Glen's funeral, I learned more about how he left this life. His family members told me that in his final hours, Glen moved in and out of consciousness. He'd slip away, then he'd come right back and look wide-eyed at the ceiling, as though he were looking into eternity.

"Wow! Wow! Wow!" Glen said over and over, as he was viewing the other side. Then he began to sing.

In his last moments, Glen started singing one of his favorites, "What a Day That Will Be."[3] When he got to the part of the song that says, "When He takes me by the hand," Glen lifted his hand to sing (like so many of us have seen him do onstage) and as he did, he took his final breath.

Do we miss him? Yes. Do his family members and friends grieve the loss of such a great man? Of course. But we don't grieve as those who have no hope.

You can see it in the faces of Glen's family. Hope! The blessed hope that what Glen sang about—what Glen lived all his life—is true! We shall see Jesus in all of His glory!

Glen had always said that when he died, he wanted to go out of this life singing about Jesus . . . and he did!

> Never be afraid to trust an unknown future to a known God.
>
> —Corrie ten Boom

22 Jessy Dixon Won't Tell

I WAS DRIVING TO THE RECORDING STUDIO today to pick up the CD our producer always makes, just for me, when we're in the process of recording a new Gaither Vocal Band project. Guy Penrod sings the baritone part for each song. It's a baritone solo, no other parts on it. I memorize it like it's the melody and pretend Bill, Guy, and David are my background singers. I can't wait to show our producer what he did, though. It's hilarious. He accidentally mislabeled my CD. It says, "GVB for Dummies."

Well, anyway, on my way, I passed George Hairr's recording studio, "The Mission House." George was cutting vocals on Jessy Dixon. When I walked in, there was ol' Jessy—dancin', singin', and in the Spirit. It was fantastic.

While Jessy was wailing, jiving, and bouncing to the music, I was thinking. *How old is he?* You see, I've been trying to find out how old Jessy is for quite some time now. And he ain't tellin'. Nobody knows. So, I've had to do some private investigating . . . nothing illegal . . . at least, not as I define it. So far, I've turned up nothing, and I've asked everybody.

Jessy Dixon and me

One night after a concert we were headed to the airport, and I was sitting next to Jessy in the taxi.

I asked him how old he was.

He said, "We don't tell."

I said, "Who don't tell?"

He said, "My race doesn't talk about it. I never knew how old my parents were. We never discussed it."

I said, "Well, you must be at least sixty."

You should've seen the horror on his face. "I am not sixty!"

I said, "As far as I'm concerned, until you tell me your age . . . you, my friend, are at least SIXTY!"

Really I don't care how old Jessy is. But when I realized he wasn't going to tell me, "the kid" in me came out. I just had to know. But after all this time, I still don't have a clue. I don't even know if he knows how old he is. Maybe his parents never told him.

It's kinda cool when you think about it. 'Cause, if you don't know how old you are, you can be any age you want. I heard someone ask once, "How old would you be if you didn't know how old you were?" I'd wanna be twelve years old, so I could return those library books I've still got and won't owe anything.

When the song was over, Jessy walked out of the vocal booth. I said, "Jessy, you sing great for sixty!" He howled, "I'm not sixty, and you'd better quit telling people that." Evidently, all those people I'd asked in confidence had shared it with others so they could "pray more intelligently," and somehow it got back to Jessy.

I hate when that happens.

> Rise early. Work late. Strike oil.
>
> —J. Paul Getty's key to success

23 Whose Prayer Was That?

AT A CONCERT IN FAYETTEVILLE, NORTH CAROLINA, I had laryngitis and couldn't sing. I could talk, but I couldn't get anything that sounded like a musical note to come out of my throat. Nevertheless, in my best "the-show-must-go-on" voice, I tried to perform despite the frog in my throat. By the time I had reached the middle of my first song, I knew it would be my last.

Instead of singing, I sat on a stool and told a lot of stories. I had Anthony perform a medley of songs on the piano, and at the end of the concert, I asked the audience to sing to me "Mary Did You Know?"

A week or so after the unusual concert, I received an e-mail from a mom who expressed how much her son had been looking forward to seeing me in Fayetteville. He is a big fan of my stories, she said, and he was really excited to hear me tell them.

The mom knew I had just released my singing project, *But Seriously*. So prior to the concert, in an effort to prepare him, she had informed her son that the concert might be more singing than storytelling. But she underestimated her son's prayer power.

After the concert, the young boy said, "Mom, I prayed and asked God to let Mark talk more than he sang." (I think a lot of people pray that.) But the little boy's prayer was answered. I told stories the whole night.

In the mom's letter, she said she was writing because she wanted to thank me for strengthening her little boy's faith.

I wrote back to the mother:

> Dear Ma'am,
>
> The concert's over. Would you tell Junior to ask God if I could have my voice back?
>
> Sincerely,
> Mark

Bill must have asked me something I didn't know

24 Be Glad You Can Flush

I USED TO HEAR NANNY AND PAW PAW (my mom's parents) talk about the "good ol' days." Nanny could remember the first time she ate a potato chip and the first time she ate Jell-O. She told me stories about cowboys who used to ride through her hometown in Oklahoma, when she was a little girl, and shoot the church bell with their pistols. And Paw Paw said he could remember when Houston, Texas, had one stoplight.

I would sit for hours listening to them. I loved my grandparents. They were full of history and stories. And they would tell their tales to me over and over. And each time was as fascinating as the time before. To my little ears, their memories sounded like a fantasy world where life was simple, time moved slowly, and everybody got along.

They seemed to forget how hot it was. How hard they had to work. And what it took just to put food on the table.

For instance, if they wanted fried okra for supper, they couldn't just grab a bag out of the freezer. They didn't have a freezer. They had to buy okra seeds, plant them in a garden, hoe it, till it, water it, nurture it, grow it, harvest it, wash it, chop it, fry it, and by *that* time . . . they were really, really hungry.

Then after they finally got a belly full of okra, they had to use the facilities, which were located twenty yards off the back porch. It was a little wooden structure, just big enough for one. (Unless you were rich. Then you could afford the duplex model.) They were called outhouses. They were freezing in the winter, but worse in the summer, when your "business" better not exceed your ability to hold your breath.

One of my earliest and fondest memories of Nanny and Paw Paw is when they'd take me to the country store. I would stand in the front seat between them. (This was before child-restraint laws and even before seat belts.) We'd sing, "I've Got a Mansion Just over the Hilltop," "I'll Meet You in the Morning," "Living by Faith," and other great old gospel songs. We'd sing our way down that long country road. Houses weren't so close together back then, and we drove for miles without seeing anyone. Nothing but pastures, hills, cows, and every now and then, a white picket fence with kids playing in the yard. It seemed like we drove forever. But Nanny and Paw Paw always made it a musical adventure. I loved the singing. I loved the car ride. But I especially loved the small, mom-and-pop country store.

There were always two old men sitting on the porch playing checkers and a hound lying by the front door. And everyone treated you like family.

As soon as the car stopped, I'd climb over Nanny trying to get out and race through the screen door. As the door slapped loudly behind me, announcing my arrival, I made a dash for the old cash register because I knew right next to it sat my favorite thing . . . a big, yellow, round slab of cheddar cheese. I loved that cheese. Paw Paw would buy some crackers, three bottles of Coca-Cola (that were five cents each), some meat, a few slices of cheese, and we'd head back home. Somewhere between Sugarland and Houston, I'd hop into the backseat, crawl up under the back window, lie down, and, with a full Texas moon shining down on my little body, fall fast asleep.

Ahhhh, those were the good ol' days . . . when cheese didn't have cholesterol, soda didn't cause cavities, and you wouldn't get a two-hundred-dollar ticket for riding in the back window.

You know what? We remember what we want to remember. We all have "selective memory." Now don't get me wrong—I

Waiting on Nanny and Paw Paw
to take me to the country store

loved our trips, but they were long, hot . . . and sticky. Summers in Houston are so humid even Pentecostals won't raise their hands. And Nanny and Paw Paw's 1956 two-tone Chevy had no air conditioning. We would roll the windows down, but that just let the hot, steamy Texas air inside. And that old country store was a breeding ground for bacteria. The hound frothed like it had rabies. And the two old drunks, who were always playing checkers, should've stopped long enough to patch the holes in the screen door that let in those Texas flies that were so big they could put on their own rodeos. The meat was pickled pigs' feet. (I prefer putting my own foot in my mouth.) Have you ever gnawed on a knuckle? Now that's eatin' low on the hog. And the cheese was a big, round, unrefrigerated, slab of cheddar that ol' Bubba, the store manager, would slice for us after shooing away the flies and roaches. Bubba only had one thumb. He said he lost it when he was a kid learning how to cut the cheese. (I wonder who got that hors d'oeuvre?)

Memories are great. But, these are the good ol' days. My air conditioner is set on sixty. I have more than three hundred channels of digital television at my fingertips. With a single keystroke, I can send an e-mail around the world. I have individually wrapped slices of American cheese in the refrigerator and two bags of okra in the freezer.

Life is good.

But the main reason I know that these are "the good ol' days" is because we have indoor plumbing. Less than five feet from where I'm sitting, in a room just off the hallway, sits the latest in toilet technology complete with a Fluid Master flushing system. There's a turbo-powered exhaust fan in the ceiling and a can of extra strength heavy-duty lilac air freshener sitting on the marble countertop. Sure, it's fun to think back to the way things used to be, to get nostalgic and smile at what we had and didn't have back in the "good ol' days," but let's face it: This is the day the Lord has made, so let us rejoice, and be glad we can flush!

P. S. In my research for this book, I e-mailed my dad to ask him the make and model of Nanny and Paw Paw's car, when I was four years old. I asked one simple question, and here was his response:

Mark,

When I met your mother in 1951, Paw Paw and Nanny drove a 1949 Ford, and I drove a 1950 Plymouth. In 1956, Paw Paw and Nanny purchased a new Chevrolet. It was a two-tone, brown four-door.

That is the vehicle they drove to Florida when we took a vacation in 1960. You were eighteen months old, and Mike was about four years old.

Every time we stopped to eat and put you in a high chair, you thought it was time to potty. Your face turned red as you strained to do your job, and I mean you did a job every time we put you in a high chair. We laughed about that all the way to Florida and back to Texas.

They kept that Chevrolet until your mother and I gave them our 1962 Ford LTD green station wagon in 1965, when I bought a blue 1965 Chrysler. They kept that car until your mother and I gave them a new Ford, around 1983. The day Paw Paw drove the new Ford home, he told me that it would be the last car he would ever own, and he was right. He died five years later, January 28, 1988.

So the answer to your question is they owned and drove the 1956 two-tone, brown, four-door Chevrolet in 1962 when you were four years old.

Love,
Daddy

What can be more absurd than the prospect of locomotives traveling twice as fast as stagecoaches?

— *The Quarterly Review*, 1825

25 The Glory Hath Departed

NOT LONG AGO, the Gaither Vocal Band was scheduled to perform in Bangor, Maine; Halifax, Nova Scotia; and St. John's, in Newfoundland, Canada. We left Nashville on Delta Airlines. We got as far as Cincinnati, where we discovered that our continuing flight to Bangor was canceled. We hopped a flight to Boston, hoping we could make a connection, but they were all full. So Bill chartered two planes, and we finally arrived in Bangor in time for the concert. Unfortunately, our luggage went to Tahiti. It had a better travel agent.

We performed our entire program wearing the clothes we'd been flying in all day. By the time we got to "He Touched Me," my shirt smelled tired. Bill was wearing a bright blue suit that he found in his closet on the tour bus that met us in Bangor. But Bill's suit really didn't go with his hair. He looked like a Smurf Chia Pet.

Despite our unusual appearance, the people in St. John's were sweet. They talked too fast, but they were sweet. They also liked to kiss a lot. I know that Paul said to greet the brethren with a holy kiss, but do you really think he meant it? And what if you don't want to? And how do you know it's gonna be holy? And what's the difference?

We flew home on a private jet. The flight from Bangor to Alexandria, where Bill and Gloria got off the airplane, was as smooth as glass. No air pockets and no unexpected jolts; everything was just perfect. Then we took off from Alexandria and headed for Nashville. Janet Paschal, Guy Penrod, the pilot, and I were the only ones on the plane.

Suddenly, the beautiful, private jet became Beelzebub Airlines. We hit a major air pocket. Guy's head slammed against the ceiling, Janet screamed like someone had stolen her record money, and my life flashed before my eyes. I said, "Well, Bill and Gloria are gone, and the glory hath departed."

When we finally touched down in Nashville, I was ready to kiss the ground. Now that was a holy kiss!

Me and Guy Penrod before the turbulence hit
and the glory departed

26 Puffed Up and Shot Down

I'M SITTING HERE OPENING E-MAIL. I love reading what people have to say. Because of the amount of e-mail I receive, I've had to hire someone to answer it for me. But I try to read as much of it as I can. I thought what I would do now, as an experiment, is open random e-mail. I will allow you to hear my thoughts as I'm reading it. I will type them down and put them in brackets, so you will know exactly what I'm thinking.

Here's one:

Mark,

Thanks so much for the entertaining and inspirational evening we shared with you at the Kings Highway Church in Avon, Indiana, this past Saturday night.
<You're very welcome. It was my pleasure.>
     One minute tears were flowing from the humor as only you can do . . .
     <Oh, how nice. Thank you.>
     . . . but then, real soon, tears were welling up as

you gave yet another touching inspirational part of the program. You were magnificent . . .

<*I love that word.*>

. . . as you led up to the final song, "Mary, Did You Know." That was better than many sermons I have heard.

<*blushing* . . . >

I've got an idea . . .

<*Hmm?*>

Have you ever considered being not only a performer at Praise Gathering, but also a presenter?

<*Well, no, but* . . . >

We come each year to Praise Gathering and we have heard Gloria do presentations. You could do that!!!

<*Well, sure I could, but* . . . >

Thanks again for just being you!!!

<*Ah, there's nothin' to it* . . . *(blushing to a deeper, richer purple)*>

God certainly has blessed you and now we are all wonderfully blessed by your entertainment and testimony.

<*blushing further, head tilted, slight grin* . . . >

May God continue to bless you and may you feel the presence of God with you as you travel around the world to share His Word.

In Christian appreciation,
Fran and Jim Shields

WOW! What a nice letter. That was so sweet, Fran and Jim.

Two more fabulous reMarkables that love me.

Let's see here . . .

Oh! There's another edifying e-mail, from one of my precious reMarkables, in my mailbox. Let's see what wonderful things this one has to say.

(opening e-mail . . .)

Hey, re-Puke-able!

<What? Was there a typo in my newsletter? I'll have to check.>

Quit sending me your junk mail!

<She must've meant HUNK mail . . . common mistake.>

I'm tired of reading about your miserable life.

<Hey, I'm living it! How would you like to do that? The least you can do is read it.>

I've never heard of you and DON'T CARE!

<How can you not know of me? You're getting my newsletters.>

How did I get on this sappy list anyway?

<The sappy list gets a different newsletter; you're on the regular list.>

REMOVE ME IMMEDIATELY! YOU MORON!!!

<It's Mark, not Moron. Another typo, I guess.>

27 What Would You Ask Jesus?

I WAS TALKING TO MY MOM AND DAD the other night on the phone. I only call my parents when I've got an hour to kill. There's no such thing as a short call to Mom and Dad. You know, aging parents repeat themselves a lot. All their friends are either sick, dying, dead, or pretty sure they will be dead soon. I told my mom that there are as many babies being born as there are people dying, so get on the welcoming committee and get off the bon voyage brigade. Find some people having babies to talk about. All those death notices are depressing!

When I'm on the phone with my parents, Mom gets on one phone, and Dad gets on an extension. I'm at my house or a hotel somewhere. Mom and I are talking; Dad is just breathing.

After the usual chitchat about family, friends, and funerals that day, I said, "Mom and Dad, let me ask you a question."

Mama quickly said, "Okay."

Daddy cleared his throat, started paying attention, and said, "Shoot."

I said, "If Jesus were sitting on the couch with you—in the flesh—and you were allowed to ask Him ONE question, and He would answer you audibly, what would your question be?"

Mama wanted to know why she only got one question.

"Because that's all He has time for," I said. "I don't know, it's just a hypothetical question. If you could ask Him one question, what would it be?"

I told Daddy to go first because I knew Mama wasn't going to be able to limit it to one question. Daddy said, "I'd ask him what Mama and Daddy are doing. You know they're up in heaven doing something. I'd just like to know what they're doing."

"That's very good, Daddy," I replied. "Now go back to sleep."

Mama quickly spoke up and said, "I'd ask Him when He's coming again."

I said, "Mama! He already told you that He didn't know."

"He does by now!" she replied.

"Mama, why would you want to know that?"

"Because if He told me He was coming at noon tomorrow, I'd get to Liberty University [she teaches there] tomorrow morning and run up and down the halls screaming as loud as I could, 'Jesus is coming at NOOOOOOON!!!'"

"Jesus is coming at NOOOOOOON!!!" Daddy parroted Mama. "And do you know where you'd be when He came at NOOOOOOON? A nut house!"

So much for my parents' response to "The Question." What about you? What would you ask Him? If you got only one question, what would you ask Jesus?

I was intrigued with how other people might respond to my question, "What one question would you ask Jesus?" I decided to give the people who subscribe to my free Internet newsletter, "reMarks," an opportunity to ask. The response was overwhelming. According to actual tallies, the two questions most of my Internet friends would ask Jesus are "Am I fulfilling Your plan for my life?" and, "Lord, Why do You love us so much?"

There were a lot of good questions. Some were funny. Some were sad. Some were from children. Some were just curious. Some were thought-provoking. Here they are:

Jesus, can You help me learn the right way to play a bar chord on the guitar?

Why mosquitoes?

Why neckties?

Considering the marriage supper of the Lamb . . . What's for dinner?

What is the thing with southern gospel singers and wigs?

Why do all the good foods have to be bad for you, and why is it that all those bad foods (like spinach) are good for you . . . couldn't chocolate be one of the four basic food groups?

I'd ask him how He feels when he's portrayed in movies by non-Jewish actors who look like rock stars (or Guy Penrod).

I would like to know who my beautiful, never-been-married, red-headed, schoolteacher, thirty-year-old, committed to God, talented, singing daughter is going to marry.

Will there be comedy in heaven? If not, will there be an unemployment line for Mark?

Are You keeping your Gaither video collection up to date, and may I borrow them when I get to heaven?

Why is it that some people can eat anything (and everything) and never gain a pound . . . while others of us can take a fleeting glance at a pepperoni pizza and develop acres of new fat cells?

I would ask Him why there is so much tofu.

When are Mark Lowry and I getting married?

Is or was there life on other planets?

Did O. J. do it?

My, Lord! How could You ever love a rotten, low-down, dirty, filthy, scumbag, dirt-wad, wormy, nasty, ugly, bowlegged, crooked-toothed, selfish, conceited, proud, lustful, boneheaded, rock-brained, hard-headed, stiff-necked sinner like me?

Which miracle was Your favorite?

Why have You decided to give all the money in the world to Bill Gaither?

How can Christians be so mean?

What did it feel like being fully man and fully God at the same time and then being separated from God on the cross?

Can you make my teddy bear come to life or go to heaven with me?

I know that there are mansions being built, but will we each have our own, or will we live together with several people?

Who is going to be living in the heavenly mansion next to mine?

Will my pet dog, Rosie, be in heaven?

What will we be doing in heaven FOREVER?

Are You coming back soon, or should I start putting money away for my retirement? (I'm 23.)

Is my Daddy, who is in heaven, aware of what's going on in my life?

Will heaven be the same for everybody?

Where did You get Your ideas?

I would ask him who is the bride, and who are the "guests" at the wedding?

If God, who is omniscient, knew that Lucifer would rebel and take one-third of the angels with him, why did God allow him to exist at all?

Lord, if You would have us know and understand only one thing in our short life, what would it be?

What hurts You the most?

Why didn't You just get rid of Adam and Eve and start over?

Jesus, I have a question for You. Are my aborted children with You?

Can I come home now?

Will my brother make it to heaven to be with all of us?

Jesus, when can my husband and I have children?

What do You want me to do with my life?

Master, how can I better serve You?

*I've sung with this woman all my life. And she's still my favorite singer.
That's my mama!*

But my favorite question out of all of the hundreds I received came from someone on my reMarkables list. She said she did exactly as I had instructed everyone to do. She sat on the couch, closed her eyes, and tried her best to imagine Jesus sitting on the couch beside her. She said she just sat there for a few moments. Meditating. Relaxing. She thought of funny questions she might ask him. Like, "Did Adam have a navel?" Or, "How bad did it stink in the ark?" Then she thought that would be a wasted question. She thought she might ask why children suffer. Or why bad things happen to good people. Should she ask about the future?

But none of these questions seemed important enough to her. So she said if Jesus was sitting beside her on the couch she would ask Him, "Can I have a hug?"

I like that.

28 My Formerly Fat Friends

I WAS IN FORT WORTH FOR A CONCERT RECENTLY, and I thought I was in heaven! I ate Mexican food three times in three days. It was incredible. The best restaurant was at 1400 North Main Street in Fort Worth. I don't remember the name of the place, but for some reason I remember the address. It's owned and operated by a Mexican family. They make everything from scratch, right down to the corn tortilla chips and salsa on the table. They don't put white American cheese on their tacos or in their enchiladas; they use cheddar, the correct cheese. Nor do they put hamburger meat in their chile rellenos, like many of the restaurants do in Nashville, where I live.

You may have noticed that I take my food seriously. I'm a Baptist, and as you know, all we're allowed to do is eat.

My Methodist friend Norman Holland loves eating, too. He's six-foot-seven and has always blamed his weight on his height. He says, "I'm not too fat; I'm tall." That makes no sense to me, but that's what he says. Once, I begged him to get on a bathroom scale. He said he wouldn't do it. So I laid some cash on the counter. He snatched it up, and the next thing I saw was a blur, as the arrow on the scale whirled around and around like a helicopter, finally groaning to a halt somewhere between "Ouch!" and "One at a time, please!"

Norman has been on an herbal diet recently. A large portion of Norman is now in the sewers of Nashville. He's lost sixty pounds. Sixty pounds! Dropping sixty pounds is like losing a small child.

My friend Norman Holland,
towering over everyone

(*L to R: Joy Gardner, Norman Holland,*
and Linda Odom)

I told him to keep it up 'til it shows.

Norman didn't laugh.

I'm glad Norman is concerned about his weight, but the thing I hate most about him being on a diet is that I can no longer talk him into cooking one of his famous health-free dinners. It was worth driving across town to get to eat Norman's fried chicken, fork-hook lima beans cooked with fatback, mashed potatoes made with real butter and half-and-half, sweet tea, yeast rolls, and more real butter. Mmm-mmm. I'm getting hungry just thinking about it.

But now, the only thing on the menu at Norman's place are herbal diet pills. He has a pill for juice. He has pills for veggies, antioxidants, catclaw, grape-seed extract, and stress relief. And he even has a pill that cleans your colon. (You don't wanna stand too close to the fireplace when you take that one.) And be careful—they all taste alike. You might think you're having some juice and accidentally take one of those colon cleansers. They may taste the same going down, but they sure make different exits.

Yes, Norman's lost a lot of weight. Yes, he looks and feels better than he has in years. Yes, he's lost the aches, pains, and stiffness of being over forty years old. And he loves it when people notice. A bunch of us can be at a packed restaurant, and I'll say, "Hey, Norman! Haven't you lost some weight?"

He'll pop up like a giant jack-in-the-box, spin around, suck in his stomach, throw out his chest (and his back sometimes), finally stumbling into a position much like the Statue of Liberty, and ask, "Do you really think so?"

We all politely applaud and continue eating our cheese-cake.

The other day, I saw Wynonna Judd at the Atlanta airport. She chased me down. I followed her the whole time she was doing it. Poor girl. Looking all over the airport for me, and all along I was right behind her, following her every move. Anyway, she said she was on a diet, too. Wynonna's diet is worse than Norman's. The first week, she eats nothing but raw vegetables. The second week, she eats some healthy something-or-other (I can't remember). The third week, she eats nothing but soy. SOY!?! Can you imagine eating nothing but soy . . . for a week? That would be soy boring!

Soy for breakfast. Soy for lunch. Soy for dinner. Soy snacks with a can of Diet Soy to wash it all down. Yuck! What does she do if she has to eat out? Tell the waiter, "I'll have the boiled soy"? (Say that three times real fast.)

Scott Davis is another one of my FFF (Formerly Fat Friends). He's lost more than eighty-five pounds, and he did it the hard way. He starved himself. That's the worst way to lose weight, because you usually gain it all back. But he did it for love. He said he wasn't gonna get married until he could tie his shoes without passing out. I told him, "The second you say, 'I do,' you're gonna be looking for the buffet." Well, he got married, and sure enough . . .

But a person can't be happy AND hungry!

So all my friends are trying to get skinnier. But I have made a commitment to myself that I will NOT give in to peer pressure. I will NOT lower the standard of Baptist tradition. I will NOT mock my forefathers who understood the value of a good potluck supper and never preached on "gluttony." I will NOT bake my chicken, nor remove its skin. The day I go on a diet is the day you can pry my cold, dead fingers off my fork.

We all have an appointment with that blond guy on the television show *Touched by an Angel*. And I hope he finds me when I'm ninety-five years old, at 1400 North Main Street in Fort Worth, with a taco in one hand, a glass of sweet tea in the other, and a smile on my face.

I love a good salad . . .

and birthday cake!

29 Let's Play

MY BROTHER AND HIS FAMILY came to visit last summer. My brother has a wonderful wife, Natashia, and four great kids—Christopher, Courtney, Chad (my clone), and Chelsea. (Okay, we're from the South. We always get stuck on one letter when we name our kids. What's it to ya?)

I had recently moved into my new house, with a gigantic sugar maple tree in the backyard. It's perfect for climbing. Christopher and Courtney immediately started climbing the sugar maple the minute they got there. Chad (my look-alike—poor child—has the same size head I do, but he's much cuter . . . if that's possible) didn't take much to climbing. He was four years old and not quite ready to tackle a big, towering sugar maple that, when illuminated, looks as scary as the wicked tree in *The Wizard of Oz.*

Chad preferred staying inside and playing with toy soldiers. I don't blame him. It was cooler inside the house with his dad and me. Mike and I were having a cup of coffee and talking about my mortgage. Chad listened for a while, then with a worried look on his face, he asked, "What's a morjig?"

We knew what he meant.

Mike and I looked at each other and laughed. We didn't know what to say. How do you explain a mortgage to a four-year-old? We just looked at each other with puzzled faces, and then his dad said, "You'll know soon enough. Now go play."

Maybe the reason the Lord doesn't answer some of our questions is because He knows we wouldn't understand it if we heard it. We're not old enough. His ways are much higher than ours. And He's a lot older and wiser than us. Maybe when we're His age, He'll tell us, and we'll be able to understand. Until then, I guess we'll all just have to do the same thing—trust Him.

Now let's go play.

My nephew/clone—Chad Lowry

30 Gospel-Singin' Germs

THIS PAST WEEKEND Guy and David had colds. They were coughing, sneezing, and basically irritating everybody. The air-conditioning system on the bus recirculates the air, so everybody gets what everybody's got. There's nothing more annoying, while I'm trying to sleep, than hearing somebody hack and wheeze. It's right up there with snoring.

It should be one of the first things you learn—cover your mouth when you sneeze. My mom threw a fit if we didn't. And well she should. Now I haven't always been the poster boy for hygiene happiness. I did, once, allow myself the pleasure of sneezing freely without parental guidance. I was outside. It was a sunny day. No one was around. And it hit me. It started in my sinuses. I felt the pressure building . . . like someone had a pair of pliers on each side of my nose, squeezing until I finally blew! "Ah ah ah ahh ahhhhhchewey!" I stood amazed by the little bubbles of mucus glistening in the sun, watching them pop and fall to the ground like discarded friends.

But I expect more out of adults. They are supposed to cover their mouths when they sneeze and then wipe it on their jeans.

What's with people?

Guess what? I caught their cold. Or I may have gotten it from Vestal. Every time I see her, she gives me a big kiss, right on the lips, usually with her husband, Howard, rolling his eyes in the background. Well, when we arrived in Wichita, Kansas, Vestal was hackin' and snottin', but did that stop her from planting one on me? No! She walked over to me, all puckered up, so how could I refuse?

We kissed . . . and immediately, little germs that were singing, "Well, I Wouldn't Take Nothin' for My Journey Now" began marching down my bronchial tubes. Those germs "Walked the Dark Hills" up to my nasal passages. They no doubt felt that they were "Living in Canaan Now."

So I am now coughing, sneezing, and basically irritating everyone.

Oh, that Amy Grant—she just can't help herself!

Having a cold makes me miserable. But on top of that, I have to put up with healthy people telling me their home remedies: garlic pills, gargling with Epsom salts, lemon-honey cocktails, and espresso fleet enemas. I've heard 'em all. And none of 'em work for me. I just have to sweat it out. Besides, I prefer my espresso in a cup.

When I get up in the morning, my hair is matted to my forehead. My nose is stopped up (and when this gargantuan proboscis is plugged, it's a full-blown cold). Unable to breathe from the congestion, I had to breathe through my mouth all night, so my tongue feels like sandpaper and is stuck to the roof of my mouth.

I go to the bathroom, wipe the dried white stuff from my lips, and cough up ET. It's not a pretty sight. I felt those little mucus mongers dripping down to my lungs, where they set up shop. I coughed up green gospel-singin' aliens for a week!

Fortunately, I was able to get a prescription from my doctor, who ordered up some cough syrup that not only eased my cough, but also made me love everybody at the same time. It's powerful stuff. Pastors should keep it on hand for board meetings.

Saturday night, I told Vestal I had a cold. She grabbed me by the throat and prayed over me. I tried to agree with her. I really did. I wanted God to heal me, right then and there.

But my cold got worse. So I did the only thing I could do. I kissed Vestal.

This is how I stay so sick!

At a concert I came out singing in Vestal's clothes.
She came running out to reclaim them.

31 From Toilet Plungers to the Resurrection

ABOUT SEVEN YEARS AGO, Bill Gaither called and said I needed to move to Nashville. He said it would be more convenient for him if I lived there. Since the reason I breathe is to make his life more convenient, I moved.

My real-estate agent showed me a lot of houses in Nashville. I asked her if there were any high-rises in Nashville. I'd always wanted to live in a high-rise because I used to watch *The Jeffersons* on TV. They lived in a big high-rise. So she found one for me. It was only five stories tall, but that was high enough.

I lived in a condo on the top floor for five years. I wasn't there but a few weeks before I realized, *I'm in a nursing home.* Everybody living there was about ten years older than God. And every night you could smell Mentholatum deep-heating rub wafting down the hallways.

But it was quiet.

Seriously, they were wonderful people, and I enjoyed living there. But I got tired of having to drag luggage from the parking lot, to the lobby, up the elevator, and down the hall to my condo.

So I bought a house. One like Rob and Laura had on the ol' *Dick Van Dyke Show.* It's just one floor, with an attached garage. No more elevators. No more trekking a half-mile from the car to the condo. Just two steps, and I'm inside the door.

My new house (well, it's not actually new; it was built in 1958) has a big back porch and one of the "largest" sugar maple trees in Nashville (at least, that's what the previous owners told me), which stretches high and hangs low over the house. There must be a lot of deer living around here because I see them in the backyard in the morning (if I'm up early enough).

After I'd moved into my new house, I decided I needed some picture hangers to hang some family photos. I discovered Home Depot. I thought Home Depot was just a big hardware store. I'd never had the need to visit Home Depot. When you live in a condo, you have a maintenance man. He fixes the plumbing, electric, or whatever else might go wrong. When you buy a home, *you* are the maintenance man. You have to fix the plumbing or electric. You cut the grass. You trim the bushes. When something breaks, you gotta fix it.

On my first trip to Home Depot, I noticed their pushcarts were a lot bigger than Kroger's. These were huge. I secretly wished Kroger would have carts this size, but it's mighty big for a fella who's just coming to get some picture hangers. But I grabbed one anyway. And it's a good thing I did.

Home Depot is a "man's paradise." Everything a man could need in life is at Home Depot. If you want to build a house, you never have to leave the place. From the cement basement to the shingles on the roof, you can find it all at Home Depot.

I wasn't down the first aisle before my pushcart was full.

I had to get another one. Wasn't long before it was full, too. They have things at Home Depot you don't even know you need 'til you see 'em. I went there looking for picture hangers and left with a Jacuzzi!

I was going down the third or fourth aisle and came upon a box full of blue toilet plungers. These aren't the suction-cup type my mom always used. These are blue plastic. All one piece, with an accordion-shaped plunger. I call it my "Ronco Power Plunger." I was using mine the other day, and a guy three doors down called and said, "Thanks! What kind of plunger was that?"

Don't you hate going to someone's house for dinner and you have to interrupt a seven-course meal to ask them where they hid the plunger? Nothing will make my heart skip a beat and turn me into a Pentecostal quicker than the sight of rising water fixin' to peek up over the toilet. I hold out my hand, raise my voice (like one of those TV preachers), and shout, "O thou foul demon of toilet cloggage, I cast thee into the dark abyss of Nashville sewage from whence thou camest . . ." Of course, I'm a Baptist, and this never works.

If I were president, there would be a plunger in every pot. I love my new plunger so much I wrote a poem about it:

Plunger Cometh
by Mark Lowry

My plunger cometh from the closet
To free the things which I deposit
A plunger full of strength and beauty
A plunger that fulfills its duty
A super-plunger, made by Ronco
That stops the pesky overflow

The flow that towels can ne'er subside.
When once they're soaked, who'll stop the tide?

My plunger cometh from the closet
To free the things which I deposit
For what is life? What does it mean?
Must I live with just a dream?
A dream I have no time to ponder
A dream I must put off 'til yonder
Day where dreams and flowers grow,
No time for dreams; I must stop the flow!

But time will come when no man plunges,
For time will cease, no more free lunches
But 'til that day shall rise with dawning
I'll keep my plunger, never pawning
My plunger cometh from the closet
To free the things which I deposit.
No I won't dread, no I won't fear
How sweet to know, my plunger's near

Kinda brings a tear to your eye, don't it?

I bought a gas grill, too. You can't have a back porch without a grill.

Once I got my house all set up, I invited some friends over. And I asked them to invite some of their friends from work. I prepared my soon-to-be-famous garlic steak. I found that if you get a cheap piece of meat and put enough garlic on it, it will taste like filet mignon. Norman brought the vegetables. Brenda brought the dessert. I made sweet tea. And we had a great meal.

After dinner, we sat around drinking coffee and talking about politics. Now I'm the first to admit I know nothing about politics. But knowing nothing about something has never stopped me from having an opinion. My dad talks when he has something to say. Me and Mama talk until we have something to say—we figure if we talk long enough, something brilliant will come out.

I said, "I vote this way because I'm a Christian blah, blah, blah . . ." I was waxing eloquently. Nancy (a friend of Brenda's and soon to become a friend of mine) spoke up and said, "Well, I don't believe in God and I vote blah, blah, blah . . ." I didn't really care how she voted. All I heard was, "I don't believe in God."

This is my entire family. Of course, I'm missing. I took the picture.

I got so excited!

I'd never had one in my home before. I went around and locked all the doors, closed the windows, bolted the shades, and thought to myself, *You're going to be here awhile.*

She began to inquire about my faith. She was asking honest questions and was very interested in my answers. I told her I thought she had more faith than I did. She asked what I meant by that. I said, "It takes a lot more faith NOT to believe in God than it does TO believe in Him. It takes much more faith to believe all the order around us evolved from some gaseous belch in the universe six billion years ago than it does to believe Someone put it all together."

I told her to think about this: Order never comes from chaos unless someone puts it together.

When I look at my watch, I can pretty much assume someone put it together. There's not a farm somewhere in Japan that grows these watches. I assume someone assembled it because it has gears, screws, leather, gold, springs . . . things that I know don't just pop out of thin air. But, you're asking me to have enough faith to believe that something much more complicated than my watch, this great universe . . . did.

Look at all the order around us. The sun—if it was any closer, we'd burn up, if it was any farther away, we'd freeze. DNA—only in the last few years have scientists discovered DNA; I've had it all along. We are individually marked by God. Your thumbprint—just look at it. There's not another one like it in the world. You wanna see an original? A masterpiece? Look at your thumbprint. You are thumbody!

Do you know what's been going on in my body while I've been writing to you? My veins are working. Arteries are carrying blood away from my heart; my main arterial vessel, the aorta, branches into smaller arteries, which in turn branch into still smaller vessels that are reaching all parts of my body. In my smallest blood vessels, the capillaries (which are located in my body tissue), a gas and nutrient exchange is occurring. Right now, while I'm writing to you . . . gas and nutrients are exchanging. My blood is giving up nutrients and oxygen to the cells and is accepting carbon dioxide, water, and waste. Then it heads back to my heart.

Right now, oxygen-poor, carbon-dioxide-rich blood is returning to the right side of my heart, which is pumping it through my pulmonary arteries to my lungs, where the blood is receiving oxygen and eliminating carbon dioxide. My pulmonary veins are returning the oxygen-rich blood to the left side of my heart. And my heart is pumping oxygenated blood through the branching aorta and arteries to all parts of my body . . .

So I can live.

And you expect me to believe all that order just happened?

I don't have that kind of faith.

I have the kind of faith that when I see a black cow eating green grass, giving white milk, and brown fertilizer, I know somebody put it together.

When I see confetti on the street, I don't think it grew there . . . I know a parade passed by.

When I look out my back porch and watch my sugar maple tree toss its autumn leaves in the air, I know God passed by. I don't have enough faith to believe anything else. I believe in the big bang theory . . . God spoke, and *BANG!* There it was.

Once we realize we don't have enough faith to believe there isn't a God, we need to go on the hunt to find out who this God is. But how are we going to find Him? The best we've been able to do is send a Tonka truck to Mars. And it hit a rock named Barney and hasn't been heard from since. How in this ever-expanding universe are we going to find God? He had to find us. He had to come to us.

So if there is a God (and I don't have enough faith to believe there isn't) and He wants to make His entrance through a virgin . . . what's the big deal? He created Adam and Eve without a daddy OR a mama.

Now if I were God, I wouldn't have been born in a stable. I'd have had a big golden staircase coming out of the sky, with angels singing and seraphim swinging and Gabriel playing a Dixieland melody on his trumpet. I'd let the world know I was coming to earth, and when I get there I'm gonna kick some tail. Because I'm a Baptist! Aren't you glad I'm not God? I'm glad you aren't either.

But He was born of a virgin.

I tell you who I feel sorry for . . . the people who were asleep in the motel while God was being born in the barn. They were just a few feet away . . . and they missed it. Only Mary, Joseph, and a few barnyard animals witnessed the entrance of the King.

I believe when God came to earth, He wrapped Himself in human flesh. He set aside His omniscience: He answered some questions with, "Only the Father knows." He set aside His omnipresence: Jesus couldn't be everywhere at once. And He must've set aside His memory of who He was, too.

He didn't come full-grown. He came as a baby. Now my dad thinks Jesus knew who He was when He was a baby. I don't. And when he writes his book he can say what he wants. Like I said to Mrs. Graham, I told Daddy that if Jesus knew who He was when He was a baby, then He was faking all those diaper changes.

Jesus probably learned a lot from Mary's bedtime stories. Don't you know her bedtime stories were the best?

I've always loved bedtime stories. I'd still live at home if my dad would tell me bedtime stories. Can't you see little Lord Jesus crawling up in His mama's lap and asking her to tell Him again about the night He was born? Stories about shepherds, kings from afar, and a star in the east. Stories of angels saying, "Glory to God in the highest, peace on earth, good will toward men." And in school they were studying the Torah, His favorite subject. And every time He flipped a page . . . there was His picture. He fulfilled every prophecy.

I don't know how old Jesus was when He realized who He was. But I know He knew it by twelve, when He was visiting Jerusalem. He was teaching at the temple. His family had left for home, and they were two days into their journey before they realized Jesus wasn't with them. (That's when I knew I wanted to be a Christian. God ditched His mom for four days.) Don't you know Mary was in a panic? She was entrusted with God's kid, and she lost Him. She spent two more days going back to Jerusalem to get Jesus. And Jesus didn't have to bathe for four days. Every twelve-year-old boy would love that.

Mary finds Jesus teaching in the temple and told Him how He had worried them. He said, "Don't you know I must be about My Father's business?"

And she bought it! That line never worked for me. I tried it. My mom said, "I'll show you your father's business" as she spanked me into the house. Because my mom knew I wasn't virgin born. But if anybody knew Jesus was virgin born . . . Mary knew it. That's one thing they couldn't steal from her—her memories of shepherds, kings, and promises.

Then we don't know what happened. Nobody wrote it down. From Jesus' thirteenth year to His thirtieth . . . not a word. Good night! God's in the house! Isn't somebody keepin' a journal?

I got stuff I wanna know. What was His best subject in school? Did Mary ever make Him get a haircut? Did Joseph ever tell Him to turn the music down? Did He make His bed? Did He have chores? How much was His allowance? Was He ever grounded for something He didn't do? Did He wrestle with His little brothers? Was He hyperactive? Did He like sports? Did Mary ever walk in His room and say, "My Lord! Clean this mess up. Were You born in a barn?" Did He ever take a fish and feed the whole neighborhood? Did He perform miracles around the house? And if He didn't, how did Mary know He could at the marriage supper? Because the next time we see them, He's thirty, He knows He's the Messiah, she knows He's the Messiah, and He's still living at home. She's ready for Him to go Mess-I!

Has your mother ever said anything to you . . . and it doesn't matter what flies out of her mouth . . . you KNOW exactly what she's thinking? I believe we have one of those situations here. Mary says to Jesus, "They've run out of wine at the marriage supper." That's all she said. But He heard something else . . . they had talked about this before.

You know, if my mother came up to me and said, "They've run out of Diet Coke at the party," I wouldn't think she wanted me to turn water into Diet Coke. I'd think she wanted me to go down to 7-Eleven and buy some more Diet Coke.

But Jesus' response was, "Woman . . ."

Let's stop there for a minute.

That may be respectful in Israel . . . but if you're from Texas and call your mother "Woman," you're going to be wearing your teeth around your neck.

"Woman! What have I to do with thee?" Jesus said. What am I going to do with you? "My time has not yet come."

But it had.

This time His mama was right. It was His time. So she told the servants, "Whatever He tells you to do, do it." They filled the pots with water, and He turned the water into wine. I love that. Jesus' first miracle was one just to keep the party going!

Then He began performing all those really cool miracles— healing the sick, giving sight to the blind, legs to the lame, a new mind to the demon possessed, walking on water, feeding thousands with a little boy's lunch, and THE BIG ONE, (drumroll) raising the dead.

That one settles it . . . He had to be the Son of God.

Remember Lazarus? He was already dead. "Dying" was behind him. He was floating in paradise . . . eating dinner with Moses, Abraham, and the fathers of our faith. They were all sharing a bucket of fried chicken. He was telling his story to Esther and Ruth about how sick he'd been on earth and how awful it was to live in Israel before they had invented air conditioning . . .

But his testimony was interrupted when Jesus stood outside Lazarus's grave where his stiff, wrapped body had been entombed for four days and hollered, "LAZARUS, COME HERE!" Lazarus came hopping out of that tomb, with a "What do You want?" look on his face.

Yep, Jesus made dead men walk. He never preached a funeral. He raised the dead. When the dead sit up, the funeral's over and we can all go home . . . if we don't drop dead first.

Three and a half years after He'd started His ministry, Jesus was crucified. Why? Not for healing the sick, raising the dead, or multiplying food for the multitudes. (That'll get you a TV show.) Jesus was crucified for claiming to be God. He said, "When you've seen ME, you've seen the FATHER." The Pharisees and Saducees, the religious leaders of that day, said that was blasphemy. But, I think they knew who Jesus was. They just didn't want to relinquish their power.

So, they crucified Him, and Mary, His mother, never said a word. The silence of Mary at the cross is one of the greatest testimonies that Jesus really was who He said He was. If anybody knew, for sure, He was virgin born, Mary knew it. That's one thing they couldn't take away from her.

If I were being crucified in my hometown for claiming to be God, my mother would be pitchin' a fit. She would say, "He's crazy, but don't kill him. He's a liar, but don't crucify him. He's a lunatic, but don't take his life!" Because my mother knows I wasn't virgin born.

The first one who held Him when He entered the world was the first one who held Him when they took Him down from the cross, His mother. Then they placed Him in a borrowed tomb because He was only going to need it for the weekend. On the third day, He rose from the dead. And Mary saw it all.

I'd love to be able to sit down with Mary and, over a cup of coffee, ask her some questions. I put some of my questions down on paper a few years ago. Buddy Greene added some music and turned it into a beautiful song.

Here are the lyrics I handed to Buddy:

Mary Did You Know?

Mary did you know that your baby boy
will one day walk on water?
Mary did you know that your baby boy
will save our sons and daughters?

MARK LOWRY

Did you know that your baby boy
has come to make you new?
This child that you delivered
will soon deliver you.

Mary did you know that your baby boy
will give sight to a blind man?
Mary did you know that your baby boy
will calm a storm with His hand?
Did you know that your baby boy
walked where angels trod?
When you kiss your little baby
you've kissed the face of God.

The blind will see
The deaf will hear
The dead will live again.
The lame will leap
The dumb will speak
The praises of The Lamb!

Mary did you know that your baby boy
is Lord of all creation?
Mary did you know that your baby boy
will one day rule the nations?
Did you know that your baby boy
is Heaven's perfect lamb?
This sleeping child you're holding
is The Great I Am!

32 God's a Show-Off

I JUST GOT HOME from a great weekend in California and Arizona with the Gaither Vocal Band. I've got a great job. It's a job, but I don't really think of it as work. Not that I don't cash my checks or anything like that. It's just fun.

I feel the same way about work that Abraham Lincoln did. I just happened to find a little-known quote by the great emancipator, Mr. Lincoln: "My father taught me to work, but not to love it. I never did like to work, and I don't deny it. I'd rather read, tell stories, crack jokes, talk, laugh—anything but work."

So, I'm in good company. But I would've needed a bigger hat. I do love what I do. All I have to do is sing close to pitch and make fun of Bill Gaither's hair, to do my job. AND I GET PAID TO DO IT! I love America!

We all flew home on the same flight. Candy Christmas and I were standing at the ticket counter, and the lady checking us in recognized me. "Aren't you Mark Lowry, the comedian?" (And I don't even think she was reading it off my T-shirt, either.)

I smiled my most humble smile. "Why, yes, but I like to think of myself as a storytell—"

"Then why don't you tell us a joke!" she interrupted.

I told her, "I'd love to, but I'm off the clock."

Then Candy piped in, "If you bump him up to first class, he'll tell you one." The lady kind of chuckled (as if to say, "I've heard him . . . his jokes aren't that good").

Then Jake Hess walked up. The lady was one of his biggest fans and immediately "bumped him up" to first class.

But . . . Jake is a legend. I'm just one in training.

I don't really like first class, anyway. Those seats are too big, the food is too fattening, and if you crash, you hit first— all those poor slobs in the back piling on top of you. It could be messy. I'd rather sit in the back with all those poor slobs who will land on top of first class . . . should we crash. But I'd try to do it gently.

I had to sit on the back row, middle seat, between two people who had eaten too much. They took up their seats and half of mine. They already had the armrests up (so they could expand a little) by the time I showed up. They were using the only two extension seat belts on this flight (which meant I wouldn't get one). But all the other seats were taken, so I sat there, feeling like a ham sandwich.

The back-row seats don't recline. There's a wall that stops you. But the seat in front of me reclined like a La-Z-Boy! So there I was, squeezed between two farm-fed frequent flyers, with the guy in front of me in my lap . . . for three hours!

I got bored.

So I checked out his dental work. Other than the one cavity in the back, right molar, I think his dentist did a good job.

Finally, I squeezed back into my seat, laid my head back, closed my eyes, and tried to relax.

I thought to myself, "So? What am I gonna do now?"

I had no idea.

Then I heard what sounded like the Lord in my mind, saying, "Hey, let's talk . . ."

"Why not? I can't go anywhere. I've got three hours to kill. The deacons on each side of me ain't movin'. Sure, Lord, let's talk."

And I heard from God.

You know, that's the coolest thing—to hear from God. Sometimes I get so busy, and I'm surrounded by so many people, that it's hard to hear God in all the noise.

He doesn't holler . . . unless He has to. (And by the time you got Him hollering, you're already in a mess.) He talks to us in a "still, small voice." A "still, small voice" is hard to hear when you're whizzing by it. It's "still" . . . you're whizzing. God had put me between two sumo wrestlers. I couldn't whiz. He had my full attention.

Sometimes God gets my attention by showing off. I just looked out my office window, and He's doing it right now! I'm looking at a full moon. It's bright, it's clear, and it's right between the window frame and the blinds—the perfect spot.

If you don't think God's a show-off, then you've never seen a sunset over an ocean. I was down in Panama City at the beach a couple of weeks ago. I watched a hundred sunsets in one night. Just about the time I thought, *That was the most beautiful sunset I've ever seen,* God seemed to say, "You think that's pretty; watch this." Then He blew the clouds a little and revealed an even more spectacular one.

I just stood there in awe. Afraid if I blinked I'd miss something. I began quietly bragging on God. I told Him how creative, incredible, and magnificent He was. I said, "Go on, Lord, show off!"

And He did.

I'm just glad I didn't whiz by it.

I was very excited about the ocean

33   The Last One to the Lake Is a Rotten Egg

LAST YEAR, I flew to Lynchburg, Virginia, to surprise my sister, Melissa, for her thirty-second birthday. I told my brother, Mike, not to tell anyone. By the time I got there, Missy, Mama, and Daddy were the only ones he *hadn't* told.

The next day I went camping with Mike's family . . . not one of my favorite things. Sleeping bags, fire ants, and port-a-potties are not my idea of a good time. I would've preferred the Hilton with twenty-four-hour room service. But hot dogs, roasted marshmallows, and mosquito bites were in my future. My brother has a pop-up camper with air conditioning. So that made it bearable.

My nieces and nephews—Christopher, Courtney, Chad, and Chelsea—were all excited about the trip. They didn't even notice when the trailer-hitch ball didn't fit, and my brother had to go clear across town to get one that did. They didn't worry when we got to the campground and the pop-up camper didn't pop up. They didn't see the sweat pouring off the end of Mike's nose as he cranked the camper up and down, hoping to hear that clicking sound that would assure him the roof wouldn't fall in on us. His kids weren't sweating.

(I would've helped him, but I had this book to write. I couldn't risk throwing my writing finger out of joint.) No, the kids were in their own world—laughing, putting on their swimming trunks, and heading for the lake.

To make sure I record everything accurately in this chapter, I just finished watching the videotape of that weekend. At the end of the first day, my brother was lying on the bed in the camper watching the kids play. They were jumping and laughing, playing games, and making faces for the camera. (I don't know where they got that from.)

Every now and then, Mike would break into a big smile. He was too tired to move. He had that wide-eyed stare you get when you want to go to sleep, but you're afraid you'll miss something. He worked hard that day so his children could have a good time. That's his job. He's the dad. He's supposed to have everything under control. "When something breaks, Dad will fix it." Kids are supposed to laugh, put on swimming trunks, and head to the lake.

One afternoon, while my nephew Chad was playing just outside the camper, Mike and Natashia were inside talking about all the things they were hearing on TV about Y2K. Mike, not knowing Chad was hearing every word, said, "There could be food shortages, power outages, no water, mayhem in the streets, people killing each other, and maybe even a nuclear war. Life may never be the same." All of a sudden, Chad was crying. Mike and Natashia realized he had been listening. Natashia picked him up, put her arms around him, and said, "Chad, you don't have to worry about anything. Your mom and dad are gonna take care of everything." Chad clapped his hands, broke into a big smile, and said, "Well, that's that!" And he went back to playing.

I love that story. Listen to this:

> This resurrection life you received from God is not a timid, grave-tending life. It's adventurously expectant, greeting God with a childlike "What's next, Papa?" God's Spirit touches our spirits and confirms who we really are. We know who he is, and we know who we are: Father and children. And we know we are going to get what's coming to us—an unbelievable inheritance! (Rom. 8:14–17 MSG)

So clap your hands and say, "Well, that's that!"
And the last one to the lake's a rotten egg!

34 Don't Let Worry Kill You; Let Me Help

DECEMBER 27, 1999

I hope you had a Merry Christmas. Did you get everything you wanted? I got some knives I couldn't bring home because I was afraid I'd get arrested at the airport. But I had a great time in Lynchburg visiting with family and friends. A lot of folks back home have been reading up on Y2K . . . the computer bug that could possibly shut down a lot of stuff around the world at 12:00 midnight, January 1, 2000. I was discussing it with a good friend of mine who said he believes it will take five generations before the human race will again experience life as we know it . . . but he doesn't think we'll last that long.

It was a sobering Christmas, but I still had a lot of fun. I saw my mom and dad. I stayed a few nights with my brother, Mike, and his wife, Natashia. Had a great time visiting with my sister, Melissa, and her new husband, Charlie, and all the nieces and nephews.

I went over to Doug and Laura Lee Oldham's house and had "pannhas"—a loaf of cornmeal and liver and other foreign substances that is sliced thin, fried crispy, and eaten with mustard. It's one of their Christmas traditions, and I crash their party every year for a taste.

It was a busy, game-filled, ham-and-turkey-eatin' Christmas. Mama made her traditional pralines and divinity. Last night we saw *The Prince of Egypt*. We hadn't been home ten minutes when my brother spotted a deer out his bedroom window, grabbed the bazooka under the bed, and blew the little critter to deer-jerky heaven . . . which Mike says will come in handy during Y2K.

There are a lot of things to worry about these days. (Especially if you're a deer.) Y2K is just one of 'em. We got Iraq over there building biological weapons so she can kill "the great Satan" . . . us! Bosnia and Serbia are killing each other for some reason. Korea has nuclear weapons, so we gotta try to keep her calm. Ireland's trying to divorce Great Britain. And if that's not enough, the weather channel shows more hurricanes, volcanoes, tornadoes, earthquakes, tidal waves, floods, ice storms, fires, wars, and rumors of wars while the leader of the free world is being tried in the Senate.

I was talking with my friend Rick Dinoff about all this stuff and what some people were predicting. We were discussing how it would affect us—he, as a married man with a wife, children, and a grandbaby to worry about; me, single with nothing to worry about. (Although the food-shortage thing has me a little concerned. What is the shelf life of Ding Dongs anyway?)

I said, "It wouldn't hurt to have some extra water on hand, maybe put in a diesel generator or two in the backyard. Fill the basement with Cheerios, cans of tuna, and toilet paper, and put an outhouse in the backyard. It wouldn't hurt to strap some solar panels on your roof and store some matches, candles, and hair spray."

Just then, my friend George Hairr called. George is my North Carolina redneck fishin' buddy. He's also the Gaither Vocal Band's studio engineer. He always has something funny to say. He asked what I was doing. I said I was talking to Rick about the future. George said, "Well, that shouldn't take long . . . 'We don't know what's gonna happen' should cover it." We laughed.

When I hung up with George, Rick grabbed the Bible (he likes to drag God into our discussions) and said, "Let me read something to you."

Listen to what he read:

"Don't hoard treasure down here where it gets eaten by moths and corroded by rust or—worse!—stolen by burglars. Stockpile treasure in heaven, where it's safe from moth and rust and burglars. It's obvious, isn't it? The place where your treasure is, is the place where you will want most to be, and end up being. . . .

"If you decide for God, living a life of God-worship, it follows that you don't fuss about what's on the table at mealtimes or whether the clothes in your closet are in fashion. There is far more to your life than the food you put in your stomach, more to your outer appearance than the clothes you hang on your body. Look at the birds, free and unfettered, not tied down to a job description, careless in the care of God. And you count far more to him than birds.

"Has anyone by fussing in front of the mirror ever gotten taller by so much as an inch? All this time and money wasted on fashion—do you think it makes that much difference? Instead of looking at the fashions, walk out into the fields and look at the wildflowers. They never primp or shop, but have you ever seen color and design quite like it? The ten best-dressed men and women in the country look shabby alongside them.

"If God gives such attention to the appearance of wildflowers—most of which are never even seen—don't you think he'll attend to you, take pride in you, do his best for you? What I'm trying to do here is to get you to relax, to not be so preoccupied with getting, so you can respond to God's giving. People who don't know God and the way he works fuss over these things, but you know both God and how he works. Steep your life in God-reality, God-initiative, God-provisions. Don't worry about missing out. You'll find all your everyday human concerns will be met.

"Give your entire attention to what God is doing right now, and don't get worked up about what may or may not happen tomorrow. God will help you deal with whatever hard things come up when the time comes." (Matt. 6:19–34 MSG)

Rick closed his Bible and asked, "So, Mark, are you still worried about Y2K?"

I said, "I'm not worried about anything. Haven't you *also* read in the Book of Proverbs, 'Go to the sluggard thou busy ant' or something like that? Now get out of my way; I got to go show 'em where to put my generator."

JANUARY 2, 2000

The Y2K problem was either a fluke or they fixed it in time; either way, my worry didn't help matters. And I never did get to use my generator. But that's okay.

I'm worried about the Middle East peace talks now. I'm digging a bunker in the backyard that can withstand a nuclear onslaught, in case those post-tribbers (people who believe the Lord is coming AFTER the tribulation) are right.

And to help pay for the bunker, I've got some product I'm selling real cheap. It's my "After-Y2K Special." You'll receive my book that sold hundreds of copies in 1999: *Mark Lowry's Answer to the Coming Y2K Crisis,* my six-tape series entitled, "Whatcha Gonna Do When the Lights Go Out in Georgia?" AND you'll also get my latest solo project, *Heartwarming Songs for Nuclear Winter.*

Friends, individually, these items could sell for ninety-nine dollars. But today, you'll receive all of these fine, reputable products for only . . . oh, let's say . . . I'm feeling kind of generous . . . shall we say . . . POSTAGE! We need to make room in the warehouse for my new product line coming this fall. You'll want to be looking for my new video/book/cassette/CD/8-track series, *Don't Let Worry Kill You; Let Me Help!*

35 Like Puttin' Whipped Cream on an Onion

I'M SITTING ON THE PLANE waiting on everybody. Here they come . . . Bill, Guy, David, and George (Bill's dad). We're headed to Texas, and I'm excited! Mexican food EVERY DAY! Guy, David, and I call Texas "God's Country." Bill said, "In the summertime, God can have it."

Bill's just mad because he was born in the North and the Indiana Pacers got beat last night. He said he didn't want to talk about the game, and now that's ALL he's talking about.

We're all settled in our seats. So, I thought this would be the perfect time for me to ask a few questions. Many people have asked me why Guy doesn't have e-mail. So let me ask him . . .

"Guy, why don't you have e-mail?"

GUY: "All that Internet stuff is too overwhelmin' to me. With four boys to chase through the woods, I don't have much time to . . . how do you say . . . surf the net? I still have a P. O. box, but I'm not real sure what the number is. It's in town, and we don't go there much."

I continued to type, looked up, and smiled.

Wait! Bill wants to say something . . .

BILL: "Uh, uh, uh, [holding hand on top of hair] uh, well, you know, why not? Uh, uh, and . . ."

We'll get back to you, Bill.

Bill's sitting next to his eighty-five-year-old father, George, who runs three miles every morning at 5:30. I asked George why he runs, and he said he's trying to catch Lela (his wife/Bill's mom). You can meet George at the Gaither product table any night. He's been traveling and working at the Gaither product tables for twenty-seven years, since his retirement from General Motors.

As I said, there are three Texans in the Gaither Vocal Band: Guy, David, and me. Bill's the only Yankee. And you should hear what he says about us Southerners when we're up North.

Bill's saying, "No! No! No! Don't tell 'em!" And he's kicking my leg so I can'lk ;typed realt goodw.

I told Guy to hold him down while I tell my Southern brothers and sisters what Bill says about us. He says, "These boys are from the South. They don't always know how we Yankees are gonna take 'em—they know how we took 'em one time!"

HA! HA! HA! Bill, you're so funny!

Let him go, Guy.

Bill is begging me to tell you, "That's a joke I got from Hovie Lister forty-five years ago" (like that makes it right), "and the last time we were in Texas, Governor Bush made me an honorary Texan" (like that makes it right).

Bill Gaither? An honorary Texan? You might as well put whipped cream on an onion.

When Bill starts saying "y'all" instead of "you," orders grits instead of hash browns, and adds "Yellow Rose of Texas" to the program, then I will believe.

No I won't. I won't believe it until he "brings forth, therefore, fruits meet for repentance" (Matt. 3:8 KJV).

It's just too late. He's too old. You can't teach old dogs new tricks. And that old dog will be a Yankee until the day we place his dyed, permed wig on his cold, dead head and send his soul to North Heaven. But, he'll have to come down South to visit me, Guy, David, and the Lord—South Heaven, that is.

Scott Davis, Rick Vigneulle, and me—
the group I hung out with before Bill Gaither found me

I wish people who have trouble communicating would just shut up.
—Tom Lehrer

36 Give the Lord a Challenge in the Rapture

BILL GAITHER JUST CALLED. He said he's on a diet and lost fifteen pounds since I've last seen him. I asked, "Did you get a haircut?"

He said, "No, I'm losing weight by eating vegetables." I asked if he was allowed to cook 'em in fatback and bacon. He said, "I don't even like the taste of ham in my green beans anymore." Well, la-di-da!

He went on to tell the colonic benefits of eating vegetables. We talked about everything from regularity to age spots. It was a pleasant conversation. You know you're officially over forty when you can spend thirty fascinating minutes talking about polyps.

I asked him what he ate today. He said, "A slice of wheat toast in the morning, cottage cheese and fresh tomatoes at noon, then green beans and a salad for dinner."

So, I asked him again, "What did you *eat* today?" He repeated himself, which he does often, but it sounded like a snack spread out over the day. While I was talking to Bill, I was looking at the sticky notes on my computer. And then I saw it: a meatless recipe I'd written down and tried. I told

Bill I had a dish that would go perfect with his vegetable diet. There is NO MEAT in the following recipe. Not one of God's creatures had to die for us to enjoy this wonderful side dish. Absolutely nothing in the following recipe ever had a mother.

Mark's ReMarkable Vegetarian Side Dish

Combine the following:

1 cup self-rising flour
¾ cup sugar
2 tablespoons cocoa
1 teaspoon vanilla
½ cup milk
2 tablespoons margarine (or butter if you laugh in the face of cholesterol)

Pour into baking dish. Mix together and sprinkle 2 tablespoons cocoa and 1 cup sugar on top. Pour 1 ½ cups of hot water over all. Bake at 350 degrees for 30–40 minutes. Top with homemade vanilla bean ice cream.

I'm glad Bill's lost weight. But, have you seen him lately? I don't think anyone should weigh less than their hair. And as padded people (like me) age, we have less wrinkles than skinny people (like Bill). In fact, Bill was commenting about the excess epidermis that hangs around his neck since he's lost weight. He said his grandson, Jess, was sitting on his lap the other day and started playing with his multiple chins. Jess sat quietly as he twisted and pulled on them and finally said, "Papaw, did God make you?"

Bill said, "Yes."

"Did God make me?"

"Yes, he did Jess."

Jess sat there for a minute and then said, "He's doing a whole lot better these days, isn't He?"

So, there you have it. Wanna have grandkids playing with your turkey neck? Lose weight. Wanna give the Lord a challenge in the rapture? Order a pizza. God can handle it.

> I refuse to spend my life worrying about what I eat. There is no pleasure worth forgoing just for an extra three years in the geriatric ward.
>
> —John Mortimer

37 You Might Be Hyperactive If...

YOUR PLAYPEN HAD ELECTRICAL FENCING.

Your youth pastor ever gave you the wrong directions to camp.

Your baptism took more than four minutes underwater.

Your baby-sitter wears full body armor.

You're in the principal's office so often, you feel you should be put on the payroll.

A church usher has ever mentioned your name and exorcism in the same sentence.

Anyone ever put Krazy Glue in your highchair.

You've ever thought about bungee jumping off the church balcony during the invitation.

Your parents have ever been more than two weeks late picking you up at Grandma's house.

You've ever wondered what it'd be like to ride a ceiling fan.

Your pets are in therapy.

You were ever the reason for a teacher retiring.

The only time you know you'll be able to sit still in church is at your funeral.

You consider a nap cruel and unusual punishment.

You have no clue, whatsoever, when your parents have "had enough."

For the first five years of your life, you thought your name was "Be Still."

Your mother ever gave you cough syrup when you weren't sick.

Your bedroom door locks from the outside.

A pilot has ever asked you to quit rocking the plane.

Your parents went gray by your third birthday.

You consider heavy metal lullaby music.

Your tricycle has a V-8 engine.

> If Abraham's son had been a teenager,
> it wouldn't have been a sacrifice.
>
> —Scott Spendlove

38 How Did We Live before Christmas?

How Did We Live before Christmas?
by Mark Lowry, Christmas 1989

Christmas comes but once a year
But what if it came more often?
It would bankrupt the economy
Snow would surely wreck the ecology
Kids would sing "Jingle Bells" 'til we're up a tree
And drive us to an early coffin

Christmas is a yearly thing
And I'm really glad that it's so
If it came around every other week
We'd be so tired we could hardly speak
Our checkbooks would be up a creek
We'd have to shorten ol' Santa to just one "Ho!"

Yes, once a year it rolls around
It comes every month of December
Bringing cheery songs with cheery rhymes

And shopping sprees that pass the time
We have to stand in those weary lines
There's always someone I forget to remember

But think with me, for just a while
Of the years before there was Christmas
The time before the Christ child came
The time before the angels sang
The time before we knew His name.
How did we live before Christmas?

Did little children ever sing?
Did silver bells refuse to ring?
Did hosannas ever crown the King?
How did we live before Christmas?

Did winter's chill make faces glow?
Did lovers kiss 'neath mistletoe?
Try as I might, I'll never know.
How did we live before Christmas?

A virgin delivered the blessed gift
Of Christmas to the world.
All heaven wrapped in swaddling clothes
Pure deity from head to toe
Who left His throne so all could know
The glory and wonder of Christmas

So Christmas isn't gifts and toys
Or waiting on Saint Nicholas.
Christmas is a Savior's birth
A gift from heaven sent to earth

To show the world what each heart is worth.
How did we live before Christmas?

> Three stages of a man's life:
>
> He believes in Santa Claus.
>
> He doesn't believe in Santa Claus.
>
> He is Santa Claus.
>
> —Author Unknown

39 The Cool Spot

MY FIVE-YEAR-OLD NEPHEW dipped his cookie in his milk and proudly announced to the entire room of relatives, "I have a wonderful life, don't I?"

I spent the last few days with my family in Virginia. I got home last night, watched a little TV, and tried to go to sleep. I was just about to doze off when my mother called to make sure I got home all right. When I'm in that stage just before deep sleep and I get awakened, I spend the rest of the night looking for "the cool spot." (Those of you who toss and turn at night know "the cool spot" is the most important part of the bed.)

Finally, I got to sleep. Then around 3:50 A.M., I woke up. I tossed and turned, thinking about all I had to do. I would leave tomorrow for twelve days, and there was a lot I had to do before I left. I also forgot three radio interviews yesterday, so I had to think about that awhile. *Somebody knocked over one of my stereo speakers while I was gone. I have to get that fixed.* (That deserved a toss.) *I have a pile of bills on my desk I need to move to the other side of the desk until there's money to pay them.* (Two more tosses.) *I have to pack.* (Move my foot to a new cool spot.) *I have to wash my underwear before I can pack it.* (Toss.) *I have to write letters to people who have written me.* On and on it went.

I tossed again to another cool spot.

I decided, "I am never going to move from this spot for the rest of my life." I'd tossed enough. If I never fall asleep again at least I'm safe. I'm under the covers. I'm on "the cool spot," and I'm going to enjoy it . . . forever. I'm not moving again as long as I live. I've heard Gloria Gaither talk about "enjoying the moment," and I plan on enjoying this cool-spotted moment for the rest of my life. I'm not moving!

When they find me here after failing to make the flight Wednesday, they'll put me in an insane asylum where I'll never have to be responsible for anything again as long as I live. There's just too much to do in one day. I can't get it all done. I'm tired. And the list of things "to do" won't let me sleep.

I waited as long as I could . . . it got hot . . . so I tossed to another cool spot.

"Be anxious for nothing, but in everything give thanks," crossed my mind. I knew that was in the Bible somewhere. But at the time I couldn't remember where. I've since looked it up. "Do not worry about anything, but pray and ask God for everything you need, always giving thanks. And God's peace . . . will keep your hearts and minds in Christ Jesus" (Phil. 4:6 NCV).

That's what I am. Anxious. Worrying about things that aren't even here yet . . . like morning. Like . . . getting up, going to the office, and meeting the day. And I realized, lying there on "the cool spot," that this moment was the only moment in time that mattered. So I could relax and enjoy "the cool spot" because this is ALL I have right now. I don't have the future. I'm not even promised a future. I have right now. This moment. On "the cool spot." God has not promised us tomorrow. In fact, I don't even have to give God tomorrow. I can't give to God something I don't have. All I can give Him is this moment. This day. This heartbeat.

I don't have to lie awake worrying about my past because it's under the blood. And Jesus will never remind me of what's under the blood. And I don't have to worry about the future; it's under His control. So when the accuser comes around holding up my past, I know it's not the Lord. I can just roll over, find "the cool spot," and say, "Oh, it's only you" and go back to sleep.

The past has been played; the future may not even show up. And it would be a shame to waste a second on "the cool spot" of the bed worrying about something that may never happen . . . like having to get up in a couple of hours.

So, the next time I'm lying on "the cool spot" worrying about tomorrow, I'll just remember what my nephew said: "I have a wonderful life, don't I?"

> In spite of the cost of living, it's still popular.
> —Kathleen Norris (1880–1966)

40 The Irony of It All

WHAT IS FUNNY TO YOU? Ask one hundred different people, and you'll get one hundred different answers. What was funny to my grandparents wasn't always funny to me and vice versa. Bill Gaither is always telling jokes that aren't funny. But it's part of my unwritten job description to tilt my head, give eye contact, slightly smile (as if I'm actually listening), and laugh when it seems he has finally gotten to the punch line. But he thinks he's funny. And all the other people around him laugh, so they must think he's funny. Unless they're on the payroll.

Have you ever had a little kid tell you a joke? He stands there, twisting his shirt, stammering, "Why, uh . . . why did the chicken cross the road?"

You know the answer. In fact, you know many answers to this age-old question. And none of them are very funny. But Junior hasn't been on this earth long enough to have heard them all—to be worn down by the question. You think to yourself, *I couldn't care less why the chicken crossed the road.* But you, of course, would never say that to a child. So you smile and ask, "I don't know, little boy. Why did the chicken cross the road?" And you wait, and you wait, while he stammers, stutters, and continues to twist his shirttail in knots . . . trying to remember the answer. You finally blurt out, "Because he wanted to get to the other side?" He says, "No, no . . . wait, uh, uh, well, yeah that's it . . . to get to the other side. You heard it already!"

People are always coming up to me wanting to tell me a joke. They'll say, "Hey, Mark, have you heard the one about . . ." And they continue to tell a joke I've already heard from Bill. When they're finished they'll say, "You ought to use that on Vestal." Or Jake or Hovie or Bill or whoever.

But what makes something funny?

I think it's irony.

If I were to walk down the street and see the pope playing hopscotch, I might find that a little funny, because I have lived long enough to know the pope is too dignified to be on the street playing hopscotch. But, if my little nephew saw the pope jumping and hopping around, he wouldn't think it was funny; he would want to join him. You see, he hasn't lived long enough to know that the pope doesn't play hopscotch. At least, not in public.

Here's another question: What is funny to God?

If the bottom line in humor is irony, what is ironic to God? Have you ever thought about it? Surely God has a sense of humor because of all the proof in nature. He created Bill Gaither . . . that's funny! He also created other creatures that are funny, such as monkeys, giraffes, anteaters, and guests on *Jerry Springer.*

Surely God can outdo anything a human mind could think up. He's smarter than Einstein. He's richer than Bill Gates. He sings better than Pavarotti. And he's got to be funnier than His funniest creature.

So what is ironic to God? Surely not a story about a blind man who finally sees; that wouldn't be ironic to God because it is in the realm of possibilities for Him. Not a tale about a man who walked across the water to visit his fishing buddies, because again, that is possible for God—He's already done it once.

So, what is funny to God? If He were going to tell a joke, what would it be? After He leaned over the battlements of heaven and whispered to Gabriel, "Blow your trumpet; I've got a joke to tell," and we could miraculously be transported to His throne, what would we hear? Would we understand it? Or would it be so ironic we couldn't comprehend it?

There's only one thing I can think of that must be ironic to God—He sent His Son to die on the cross for us. He rose again on the third day so we could be free. And some people still reject Him. That's tragic.

I guess the bottom line to humor and tragedy is irony.

> Somewhere on this globe, every ten seconds, there is a woman giving birth to a child. She must be found and stopped.
>
> —Sam Levenson (1911–1980)

41 Bill Gaither's Non–Heart Attack

IT WAS FRIDAY MORNING. I got a call from Barry Jennings around 10:30. (Barry is Bill Gaither's son-in-law and CEO.) He said that Bill had been experiencing chest pains and was going to have to have an angiogram.

"An angio-what?" I asked. "What is that?"

Barry said, "The doctors are going to have to shoot dye up Bill's veins and see what's happening with his heart."

I said, "Well, tell them not to get any dye on his hair. It's already a color not found in nature."

"It's not that kind of dye, Mark," Barry replied.

The angiogram showed that Bill needed to have an angioplasty. One of his veins was 90-percent clogged. All of the others were wide open and flowing butter. But the one on the back of his heart needed some attention. I wondered if it was because of all the fried chicken he'd been eating since I joined the Gaither Vocal Band.

Actually, Bill is very conscientious about what he eats. I think therein lies the problem. He eats oatmeal every morning. That stuff'll clog a toilet! I'm sure it's not good for your veins.

Anyway, Bill had his surgery, and everything's fine. He's

feeling great. All of his veins are now 100-percent open. And he did not have a heart attack. The doctors discovered the potential problem and caught it early.

Along with the news of Bill's heart problem, Barry also told me I was going to have to host the Homecoming concerts that weekend in Jonesboro, Georgia, and Omaha, Nebraska. Now that news nearly caused me to have a heart attack!

I was shaking! How was I going to tell thousands of people that Bill wasn't coming? These people came to see "Bill Gaither and his Homecoming Friends."

I thought back to when I had a bout with pneumonia. The international relief organization, World Vision, invited me to visit Haiti and film some video footage for their upcoming telethon. I couldn't pass up that opportunity. I was excited about being able to meet the children the ministry is helping—and especially excited about meeting one of the children I helped support but had never met. During the weeks prior to the trip, I talked to several people who had been on similar trips. One person said, "Mark, this trip will really change your life."

I said, "Great! I could use that."

I had to get my body ready for the trip. No, I didn't start doing push-ups or running a mile every day, but I did have to get some preventative medication. Since malaria is rampant in Haiti, and since I don't really care for malaria, I started taking pills well in advance of my departure date to prevent me from contracting the disease. I had to go to the local Center for Disease Control office to get the proper prescription. The doctor was real encouraging. She said, "You shouldn't have to worry about hepatitis B, because if you're careful, you probably won't get that. But," she said, "you really should get the typhoid shot."

I felt certain that all I needed was the malaria pills. But she was a young, new doctor, and she was trying to act all grown up with that prescription pad, so I thought I'd go ahead and let her sign me up for typhoid prevention, even though I really didn't need it.

Next thing I know, my pants are down around my ankles, and she's sticking needles in my hiney. I didn't know she signed me up for that!

Well, I had a cold when I got the shot. And I guess since I was already sick, the shot threw me straight into pneumonia. I called Bob (my office manager) and asked him if he could recommend a good family doctor. I didn't have a doctor because I hadn't been sick in years. Bob recommended his doctor, and I went to see him. Guess what my new doctor's name is?

Dr. Gaither! I'm not kidding. Thankfully, he's no relation to Bill. Dr. Gaither took an x-ray of my lungs and told me I had pneumonia. "Mark, you need to go home and go to bed."

"I can't, Dr. Gaither," I told him, "I have to leave town to go out with the Gaithers."

Dr. Gaither looked confused.

I said, "Bill Gaither doesn't understand the word *sick*." In fact, the weekend before my appointment, Guy Penrod was throwing up and had diarrhea (I thought long and hard trying to figure a better way to say that, but I don't think there is one), and he still sang! So Bill wasn't going to let me take time off for a miserable little case of pneumonia!

And, you know what? He didn't. I called Bill and told him what Dr. Gaither said. Without missing a beat, Bill said, "So does this mean you're gonna fly or ride the bus?"

So, when I heard about Bill's heart condition, I called Bill up and found him in his hospital room. I said, "Hey, Bill!

Does this mean you're gonna fly or ride the bus?" He laughed.

I asked it again.

He tried to explain to me how this wasn't apples and apples.

I said something like, "Oh, yeah?"

I filled in for Bill that weekend. But I didn't like it. I was scared to death. My mind was racing. I was in a dilemma. Barry was asking me to tell all those people in Jonesboro and Omaha that "Mr. He Touched Me," "Mr. Video King," "Mr. Never-Missed-a-Concert-in-Forty-Years" wasn't going to be there. I was shaking. We weren't just missing one of the Homecoming singers—one of the groups or one of the soloists—we were missing the hub. We were missing the person around whom everything turned. Our coach was sick.

Should I do it? Should I resign? Should I run away and hide?

To help me make my decision, I asked Barry, "If I do the emcee work for the concert, is there any extra money in it?"

"No, Mark, no extra money," Barry replied.

I did it anyway. It would look good on my résumé.

The Goodmans, Jake Hess, The Martins, Janet Paschal, the Gaither-less Vocal Band, Bob Cain, and Ben Speer all did a great job. I've never heard any of them sing better. They all came to the plate and hit a home run. Of course, Bill had written down the songs he expected us to sing, in order, and had it faxed to me from his hospital bed. Ben Speer laughed when I told him Bill had sent me a program. Ben said, "Even from the hospital bed, he's still programming the concert."

And Bill saw it all. Without telling us, Bill had somebody videotape the concerts and bring it to him. He called me a few days later while he was watching the concert videos.

He's a sneaky, little sick one. But he was also quick to acknowledge the extra effort everyone had exerted. Bill said he was very proud of all of us.

I told him it was the best Gaither concert I'd ever been to. He laughed, so I said it again.

He said something like, "Oh, yeah?"

> If you look like your passport photo, you're too ill to travel.
> —Will Kommen

42 Haitian Nation Inspiration

CONTRARY TO RUMORS, I didn't die in Haiti, although I did have pneumonia prior to the trip, which made me feel as though I was dying. Nevertheless, I got over the pneumonia and had an eye-opening time among the Haitian people. I've never seen such poverty—people bathing and washing their clothes in filthy streams that run in front of their little shacks, donkeys hauling stuff everywhere, ladies carrying heavy bags with bowls on their heads, piles of trash on cluttered streets, and dirt, debris, and decay everywhere!

The first night we stayed at the nicest hotel in Port-au-Prince. In the United States, this hotel might be known as "Motel 2 ½." But for Haiti it was plush. The air conditioning didn't come on until eleven o'clock at night, when the city turned on the electricity. (The government arbitrarily decides when that will be, and then only for eight hours at a time.) The remainder of the day the hotel used a generator, but only for lights, not air conditioning.

I was raised in Texas. People will go without food before they'll go without air conditioning. You can actually live longer without food in Texas than you can without air conditioning. And, Haiti is HOT! Even hotter than Texas!

They informed me, after we arrived, that we had a six-hour drive the next day to the ministry project, where I would meet my sponsored child, Nesly.

I had NO idea what was ahead of me.

First of all, it wasn't six hours; it was eight . . . which made it sixteen hours round-trip. We averaged ten miles an hour because of the roads. To call anything a "road" in Haiti is a major stretch. What they really have are non-road donkey paths. Rocky, muddy, river-crossing trails. (I don't mean crossing over the river; I mean crossing through it.) The four-wheeler in which I was traveling was a lot like being in a rock tumbler. The road (for lack of a better term) was dirt, rocks, dried-out or flooded creek beds, mud, and dust. Very little was paved. And what was paved had decayed to such a point it was mostly potholes, rocks, and rubble. We had four flat tires and then got stuck in knee-deep mud.

And that was just the first day.

We had four flat tires in one day!

Clay Crosse and me in the van on the bumpy roads of Haiti.
I'm the carsick one on the right.

While we were stuck in the mud, something unusual happened: People came out of the bushes, seemingly from nowhere, carrying the same crude hoes they were using to till the dry ground. They dug right in and helped us out of the mud.

The Haitian people are very gracious and kind, and they have the brightest smiles you've ever seen. Beautiful people! They know nothing about deodorant, however, but you get used to it after a few days. Before long, you can't tell if it's them or you!

Our drive to the ministry project took forever, but it was an interesting feast for the eyes! The sixteen-hour journey was like watching a three-dimensional panoramic movie of life from some other planet. I recognized nothing. I related to nothing. I couldn't imagine such poverty. Mile after mile. Hut after hut. The faces changed, but the plot stayed the same. I strained to look into their eyes and imagine what their lives must be like.

Under the blaring Haitian sun life seems so harsh, so desolate, so uninviting. But at night, everything changes. There's no TV and very little electricity, so the people go to bed shortly after dark and are up at daylight. They line the streets at dusk, preparing what little food they'll have that evening and sharing it with their less fortunate neighbors.

On nights when they have nothing to eat, others share with them. It's a nightly block party. And it happens every night.

Unfortunately, they speak French, and I don't. I would've jumped right out of the van and joined their fun had I known French. Haitians are enthusiastic and expressive people. At least these seemed to be. They looked like they were having fun—and not a sign of electricity anywhere. They were all talking about something. And it was very important. Yard after yard, neighbor after neighbor.

Trying to make the kids in Haiti laugh

The whole town was on the street. The kids were playing games with sticks and rocks, and the parents were sitting around fires on their front porches cooking and talking with each other. The suppertime flames flickered down the road, creating crude street lamps. I rolled the window down and strained to hear what they were saying. They were all talking at once. Children laughing. Babies crying. Men telling jokes. And

Me and my sponsored child, Nesly

mothers watching over everybody. I wanted to remember their faces as the flames flashed, and my mind took a mental picture. I could hear their loud, strong voices and see their white teeth sparkling, hands flying around their dark faces as they told their tales. Then in the next yard, heads thrown back in laughter, people slapping each other on the back. I didn't understand a single word. But I know what I saw . . . community . . . family . . . people taking care of each other.

We finally arrived at my sponsored child's home. Not surprisingly, he was extremely poor, like the rest of the country. A strapping, fourteen-year-old boy, Nesly lives with his uncle, aunt, grandma, and many cousins. The thatched-roof shacks they share are about the size of a small American bedroom. Nesly's uncle is a farmer. That's how he gets enough food to feed his family. Nesly's grandma is eighty years of age and blind. She has a little one-room shack not far from the family's. Nesly sleeps in her shack.

I played soccer with my sponsored child and his classmates. I should say, I played at soccer and for only about two minutes. By then, I nearly had a heart attack and had to quit. I'm out of shape and proud of it. Coupled with the fact that I was getting over pneumonia, and it was so hot you could fry an egg on my chin, my stamina was in short supply.

Later, I got the kids singing. Of course, they speak French, so my communication was limited. They did understand my goofy faces. They tried to make the twisted-lip face I'm known for. They knew a lot of religious songs, but I'd never heard of any of them.

I was trying to get them to sing "He Touched Me" so I could tell Bill, but they were staring at me like I just got off a spaceship. Clay Crosse (who also went on the trip) tapped me on the shoulder and said, "Let's try the Macarena."

They knew that one! They all started doing the Macarena. I got into it. I mean, I cut a rug. I'm not saying I was on the rhythm, or "in the pocket" as they say, but I had a good time. I was the Macarena Maniac.

I took my fake, ugly teeth with me, and when I put them in my mouth, the Haitian kids loved it. But while I was playing soccer, I fell. My ugly teeth, which were in my pocket, were shattered. But the children laughed with glee when I fell. Hearing their laughter was worth losing my ugly teeth.

Perhaps the main thing I discovered while in Haiti is how spoiled I am. Okay, so you knew that. My Haitian trip reminded me that I should be more thankful. There are so many things I have taken for granted in the past—the opportunity to eat anytime I want, an air-conditioned home, a hot shower, clean sheets, a roof over my head, the ability to pay taxes, and a government that is a long way from perfect and at times downright stupid, but is still the best thing going.

And right near the top of my new list of things for which I am grateful: paved roads. When we got back to the U.S., I was amazed by our pavement. It's so smooth. I wanted to kiss it.

Wish I'd learned to swim

43 A Poem to Mom

JUNE 24, 1983, MY 25TH BIRTHDAY

Today's my birthday,
My twenty-fifth,
And usually I'm the one
Who gets all the gifts.

I thought it'd be nice,
Just for a change,
To give you a gift
That's a little deranged.

Been twenty-five years
Since the day I met ya,
And it'd take twice that long
Just to forget ya.

Today I remember
The times we've had,

LIVE LONG AND DIE LAUGHING

I remember them all,
The good and the bad.

Remember the days
You'd change my diaper?
Just a stinkin' mess
And you'd have to wipe 'er.

The time Mike and I
Had a fight by the faucet?
You ran in your bedroom
To cuss in the closet.

"I've failed! I've failed!"
Was your tearful cry.
But you'd always forgive me,
As you beat my hide.

Remember the letter
I wrote in sixth grade?
And all the trouble
That sweet letter made?

They gave this ol' boy
A three-day vacation.
But dad turned that party
Into pure isolation.

I'll never forget
What ol' Daddy said,
As he beat my tail
While we circled the bed.

"A lawyer's advice,
I'll give to you, Mark,
'Cause I think that your bite's
Not as big as your bark,

If you're gonna write
A letter like that
Don't sign your name;
You smart-aleck brat."

Upon graduation,
I left with a smile,
To Virginia, and mountains,
And college awhile.

I thought the distance
Would keep us apart.
I turned around once
And there you were parked!

You came to Lynchburg
For business, you see.
But Virginia and tacos,
They just don't agree.

Mama you've always
Been good with the money.
Dad says, "You're good
For a tax write-off, honey."

Well, Mike has been great,
And Missy's just grand.

LIVE LONG AND DIE LAUGHING

Dad's the best daddy
Throughout the land.

But of all the mothers,
The good and the bad,
You've been the best mama,
A boy ever had!

Love,
Mark

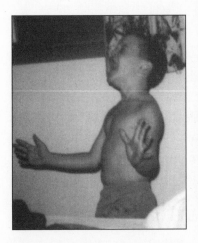 

Before . . .

After . . .
(Aren't you glad I wear
clothes now?)

44 God Loves Doubters, Too

A FRIEND CALLED and read me the lyrics to a song that was written by Kyle Matthews. It was incredible. I called Kyle, and we talked about philosophies, doctrines, and reasons for doing what we do. We talked for several hours about God and Christ and grace and deliverance and freedom. Kyle was raised in a Baptist household, too. Like me, he's from Texas, and he's curious about God. I love to talk with people who are curious about God . . . people who have more questions than answers.

I don't think God is intimidated by our questions. I don't even think He has much trouble with our doubts. He said in Isaiah, "Come, let us reason together." Wow, can you imagine trying to reason with God? Have you ever talked with someone who is infinitely smarter and wiser than you are, yet they consider your puny ideas and words important? Think of it: Almighty God invites us to reason with Him, and He is willing to condescend to entertain our ideas and comments and to discuss our questions and doubts.

When I first heard that J. D. Sumner had died, this thought popped into my mind: *I hope I told him right.*

It's easy to sit in a La-Z-Boy, talking with one of your heroes, telling funny stories between statements of faith, hope, and grace. But, when the fella dies, there's no more time to "get it right" or to explore other points of view. The questions are over. Hopefully, the conclusions we came to were correct.

I remember reading *The Grace Awakening* by Chuck Swindoll. That book is a marvelous glimpse into the grace of God. As I was reading it, I'd try to tell J. D. all that I was learning. J. D. only had an eighth-grade education, but he was educated by life beyond his years. You never had to have a dictionary around to know what J. D. was talking about. He could make it very clear. He could "put the cookies on the lower shelf," so to speak. And when we discussed God's grace and other spiritual concepts, it was so wonderful to watch the truth dawn on J. D. as he thought it through. I could see it in his eyes. I watched as his mind opened up to the wonder of it all. It was amazing. In the process, it was as though I was learning about grace all over again myself—the glory of it, the risk of it, and just how big it is.

Shortly after J. D. died, Bill premiered his new video, *Singin' in My Soul,* at the Ryman Auditorium. About halfway through the video, Tanya Goodman-Sykes sings, "Look for Me," a song written by her dad, Rusty Goodman, a long-time gospel singer who passed away several years ago. Besides being Tanya's daddy, Rusty was Howard Goodman's brother. After Tanya finished singing, Howard spoke poignantly about his own struggles. Howard confided that the devil had been coming into his room at night and making him question his faith. The devil pummeled Howard with doubt-inducing questions: "Are you sure this is all true? Is there really a heaven? Do you really think you'll see your family again?"

Howard admitted his doubts. But, he said, because of our time together singing about the Lord, it had reassured him once again that the gospel is true.

Then Roger Bennett grabbed the microphone and told us when he first learned he had cancer, he saw himself, in the future . . . on his deathbed . . . wondering, "When I close my eyes, will it be oblivion or the New Jerusalem? But I must trust Jesus just like a child."

Do you know that God loves doubters? He really does. God is not shaken by our questions or our uncertainties. He is not put out by our honest doubts when we just can't figure out the answer.

I'm fascinated when I meet someone who is so sure of everything and thinks they have all the big issues in life figured out. They are either a supersaint, or they are superstupid. On a good day, I'm right there with them, believing in the face of my doubts. But, some days are tough, and you have to walk by faith rather than feelings. I prefer seeing to believing. But seeing wasn't God's choice for us. He chose faith; He knew that would be a lot more interesting.

Jesus didn't reject Thomas because He was a doubter. Ten disciples told Thomas they'd seen the Master. This was AFTER Christ had been executed, buried, and dead for three days.

Thomas told them, "Unless I see the nail holes in his hands . . . and stick my hand in his side, I won't believe it" (John 20:25 MSG). Now, this boy was having some serious doubts.

And, you know what? If I'd been there, I probably would have said the same thing. I have tried to imagine, if Christ had been crucified in my lifetime, would I need to see Him to believe He'd risen? Probably. People have said they've seen Elvis, but I don't believe them.

My mama told me Christ is alive. But, that's not the reason I believe it. Hymns, sermons, and testimonies have told me all my life Christ is alive. Preachers, scholars, and even the Bible says, "Christ is risen." But, that's not the reason I believe it.

I believe Christ is alive because I actually see Him working in my heart and life. Thomas didn't believe until he had his own encounter with Christ. But neither did the other disciples. Everybody needs to have his or her own encounter with Jesus. We have to meet Him for ourselves. We can't believe in something with such eternal consequences on just hearsay.

After Thomas spoke those words of doubt, Jesus said to him, "Take your finger and examine My hands. Take your hand and stick it in My side. Don't be unbelieving. Believe."

Thomas believed. Wouldn't you?

Jesus has always had room in His heart for doubters. Remember when the disciples were on the boat and the storm blew, the ship rocked, and Jesus slept? The disciples cried out, "Don't You care that we perish?" Jesus said, "Oh you of little faith." Then He calmed the sea, settled their fears, and should've forever demolished their doubts about who He was . . . you would think. But He didn't.

Jesus told Thomas, "So you believe because you've seen with your own eyes. Even better blessings are in store for those who believe without seeing."

See that? We can expect . . . better blessings! That's why I've always said we Baptists are more blessed than you Pentecostals. You get miracles, healings, and see angels quite often. Vestal Goodman and Dottie Rambo have angels over for lunch on a regular basis. Angels never visit me, unless it's one of those "unawares" angels. But I still believe in this gospel. I believe without seeing. And Jesus said,

"Even better blessings are in store for those who believe without seeing."

I'm just kidding. God knows Baptists get more miracles than we deserve.

Hold on! The phone is ringing . . . I'll be right back.

That was my friend Terry. My friends and I have been praying for Terry to be healed of prostate cancer; he had the surgery. Well, guess what? God answered our prayers. All the tests came back negative.

Terry's doctor said this one baffles him.

Terry told him it was a miracle, and the doctor agreed!

Uh, oh!

I just witnessed a miracle. Does this mean I'm not a Baptist anymore?

I Believe, Help Thou Mine Unbelief
by Gloria Gaither

> I believe. Help, Thou, mine unbelief
> I take the finite risk of trusting like a child
> I believe. Help, Thou, mine unbelief
> I walk into the unknown trusting all the while.
> I long so much to feel the warmth
> That others seem to know.
> But if I never feel a thing,
> I claim Him even so.[1]

THE END

The two greatest gospel lyricists of our day—
Gloria Gaither and Dottie Rambo

Endnotes

Chapter 1: Live Long and Die Laughing

1. "Old Shep," words and music by Red Foley. copyright ABC/Dunhill Music, Inc. © 1935, 1963.

Chapter 2: Death Has No Sting

1. "The Old Rugged Cross Made the Difference," words and music by William J. and Gloria Gaither. Copyright Gaither Music Company.

Chapter 3: I Love to Laugh

1. To subscribe to "reMarks," Mark Lowry's free Internet newsletter, go to **www.marklowry.com**.

Chapter 14: Mediocrity Is Its Own Reward

1. "Kids Who Are Different," copyright © 1982 by Digby Wolfe. All rights reserved.

Chapter 21: Hope

1. "Lord, Send Your Angels," words and music by Suzanne Jennings and William J. Gaither. Copyright Townsend and Warbucks Music, Gaither Music Company.

2. "What a Meeting in the Air (Heaven's Home Is Not So Far Away)," Marty and Ann Phillips. Copyright Marty and Ann Phillips.

3. "What a Day That Will Be," words and music by Jim Hill. Copyright Ben Speer Music Company.

Chapter 44: God Loves Doubters, Too

1. "I Believe, Help Thou Mine Unbelief," copyright William J. and Gloria Gaither/Gaither Music Company.

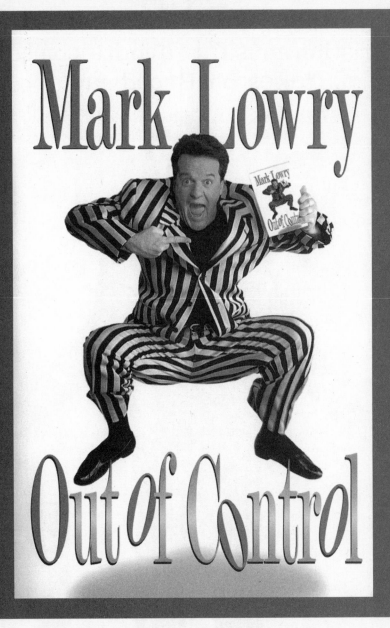

Christian music's favorite comedian takes on Broadway.

MARK
LOWRY
ON BROADWAY

Video, CD, & Cassette availabl
Sept. 26 at your favorite Christi
bookstores or by calling SpringHo
Music Group at (800) 955-874